Dedicated to my wife Anita, my two lovely daughters Marieluise and Charlotte and to all the innovators who have inspired me.

Hi!

Nice to meet you.

Editorial   Beyond the Obvious

Presentations are powerful platforms to spread new ideas, demonstrate leadership, increase visibility, and drive agendas. Every day, thousands are delivered by innovators in businesses worldwide. At their best, these presentations are informative, understandable, and inspiring. They are a crucial first step in building the future. A successful presentation educates its audience and provides a vision for the future. It enables people to make better decisions, collaborate more effectively, implement new ideas, and take action. Yet, many presentations fall short. They are often too complex and challenging to follow, confusing their audience. This ineffective communication creates a bottleneck for innovation, significantly slowing organizational transformation. Even the best idea can only effect change if it is clearly understood.

    My passion for design, innovation, people, stories, and leadership has shaped my career. Over the past two decades, I have taken on diverse roles: TV host, actor, acting coach, designer, executive coach, and creative director. This curiosity for the future drives me to teach individuals and teams how to communicate their ideas effectively. I focus on creating compelling, impactful pitch presentations and high-end keynotes. I've developed a step-by-step methodology called Agile Presentation Design to achieve this. This method has been refined over hundreds of workshops, coaching sessions, and training sessions with diverse clients, culminating in this book. Think of it as a recipe for better presentations that guides you from the initial idea to the finished product.

My process combines storytelling methods from theater and film with design principles, resulting in clear, concise, and memorable presentations. I am committed to helping my clients systematically analyze their content and distill their message to its most succinct form. This process requires in-depth soul-searching and mindful preparation, which can take days, weeks, or even months. The result, however, is a presentation that goes beyond the obvious and creates a meaningful visual experience that exceeds your audience's expectations.

Happy designing!

Ole

Content

Start

Introduction

What's the Story?
-
p. 22

Elements of a Story
-
p. 30

The Hero's Journey
-
p. 32

Three-act Structure
-
p. 34

Expert Interview: Design Thinking
-
p. 38

The Knowledge Funnel
-
p. 44

There Will Be Dragons
-
p. 46

Creative Thinking Modes
-
p. 52

The Four Formats
-
p. 56

The Five Deliverables
-
p. 58

Chapter One

Define

Expert Interview: Storytelling
-
p. 66

Presentation Strategy
-
p. 72

Communication Styles
-
p. 74

Presentation Strategy Worksheet
-
p. 75

Fabian Hemmert's TED Talk
-
p. 78

Mind Map
-
p. 80

Polar Opposites
-
p. 82

Polar Opposites Worksheet
-
p. 83

Future Scenario
-
p. 84

Visual Frameworks
-
p. 85

Future Scenario Worksheet
-
p. 87

Core Message
-
p. 88

Core Message Worksheet
-
p. 89

Chapter Two

Design

Narrative Components
-
p. 98

Rhetorical Devices
-
p. 104

Deep Metaphors
-
p. 107

Storyboard
-
p. 109

Business Pitch Storyboard
-
p. 112

Expert Interview: Startup Pitch
-
p. 116

Basic Keynote Storyboard
-
p. 120

Drawing Basics
-
p. 126

Outline
-
p. 132

Script
-
p. 133

Slide Design
-
p. 136

Visual Design Basics
-
p. 140

Handout
-
p. 144

Chapter Three

Deliver

Rehearsal
-
p. 152

Peak Performance
-
p. 156

Five Effective Ways to Calm Down
-
p. 158

A Pre-stage Warm-up
-
p. 166

Body Language
-
p. 171

How to Stand
-
p. 172

10 Strategies for a Better Stage Performance
-
p. 176

Feedback – The Real Gold
-
p. 180

Feedback Worksheet
-
p. 181

Iteration
-
p. 182

About the Author
-
p. 188

Agile Presentation Design

A step-by-step method for crafting more impactful presentations

Strategy

1 Why?

2 Who?

3 Benefits

4 Counter-arguments

5 SMART Goal

Define → Design → Deliver

Define	Design	Deliver
6 Mind Map	10 Narrative Components	17 Rehearsal
7 Polar Opposites	11 Rhetorical Devices	18 Presentation
8 Future Scenario	12 Storyboard	19 Feedback
9 Core Message	13 Outline	20 Iteration
	14 Script	
	15 Slides	
	16 Handout	

THE FOUR PRINCIPLES OF AGILE PRESENTATION DESIGN

1

Audience Centricity

Effective communication is receiver-oriented. With everything you say or show to your audience, you should always ask yourself: Does this information provide value to my listeners? You can only answer this question if you fully understand who your audience is. What are their professional and socio-economic backgrounds and their depth of knowledge; what are their interests? Gaining empathy is key to designing meaningful presentations.

2

Visual Thinking

Sketching out your ideas may be the most valuable thought exercise you can do to improve your presentation's design. Long before reaching for your computer, you should be using pen and paper to make these sketches. Our brains are set up to process visual information very effectively. Transferring thoughts into visuals will help you discover patterns in complex topics, simplify your idea and enhance your comprehension and retention.

Turning monotonous lectures into interactive experiences

3

Rapid Prototyping

An idea can only provide value once it gets out of your head and becomes tangible in the real world. This is your prototype, even if it's as simple as a quick sketch or sentence. Only once the idea is made material can it be sharpened, extended and restructured step by step. All the thoughts that follow will crystallize around this initial kernel. Don't overthink the prototype. Instead, build a "just enough" version of your presentation right away, and grow it from there. Another advantage: A prototype is a great aid for explaining your idea to others.

4

Instant Testing

The only way to find out whether your content has value is to put it in front of people right away and see how they respond. These could be your colleagues in the office, business partners at a meeting or even your wife or husband at home. What reactions, insights, questions or comments do they have? Use these to build the next, better version of your presentation.

Sharing ideas with people as early as possible to harvest their feedback greatly improves the quality of a concept.

"If you can't explain it simply, you do not understand it well enough."

Albert Einstein

Agile Presentation Design

What's the Story?

The ability to create a business presentation that captures and holds the audience's attention is one of the most powerful ways to influence behavior. People who are receptive to your message can be guided to collaborate towards a shared vision. Nonetheless, many leaders fail to ask themselves what story they want to tell before stepping in front of their audience. Without a cohesive story, the result is a dull, uninspiring presentation – highly ineffective communication.

Much has changed since 2006, when the organizers of the TED conference started making their world-class presentations accessible online. The now-famous TED presentation style takes facts and insights and delivers them as a compelling story. In the following years, this influential genre of storified presentations was further developed by Apple. The company's keynotes quickly became known for launching products and making announcements in a style that is as reduced, polished and intuitive as Apple's products.

Today, companies like Google and Facebook are also pushing the boundaries of this new form of storytelling with their annual developer events. Their presentations are professionally designed on all levels – the story, the visuals and the delivery – setting a new benchmark for all business presentations.

When Google head Sundar Pichai takes

1 → 2

CHALLENGE
-
Current situation
& interruption

STRATEGY
-
Adaptive action

3

RESULT
-
New situation &
conclusion

the stage at the annual developer conference Google I/O, he is greeted more like a pop star than a tech CEO by the 7000+ audience members. First held in 2008, the three-day annual event has grown from a niche conference for software engineers into a tech fest phenomenon with global reach and a real-time effect on the stock prices of the IT giant.

The event often feels more like a music festival than a tech conference. The program includes presentations, panel discussions and product announcements, but for many attendees the highlight is the opening-day keynote, which is also broadcast live online. This nearly two-hour presentation, led by Pichai and several other top executives, is a sort of "state of the union" address. Over the years, this event has become the new benchmark for business storytelling and presentation design: an elaborate multimedia show polished over months by armadas of skilled copywriters and visual designers. The storyline is edited to the bone, its messages crafted to be bold and catchy, the visual design unparalleled and the delivery carefully rehearsed to be approachable and laid-back.

THE 2018 KEYNOTE focused on Google's advances in artificial intelligence and machine learning, two topics that provoke strong emotions: excitement and fear. But when Sundar Pichai stepped onto the stage, he began with something unexpected: a joke. He told the audience how he fixed a major bug during the past year: correcting the position of the cheese slice in the burger emoji. He knows this kind of geeky humor will resonate in the tech community, and his anecdote was rewarded with plenty of laughs. From this opening, Pichai next spoke about how Google's

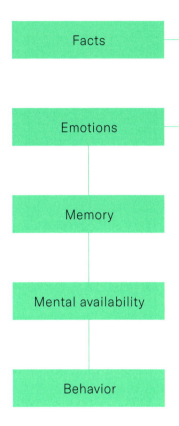

tech education initiatives have changed lives for the better, all over the world.

Why did the leader of one of the most highly valued companies on the globe open such an important public event with a light joke and stories about corporate social engagement? The answer: Because he knows his audience. He gets their values, objectives and social and cultural vocabulary.

Rather than opening with facts on Google's technological and financial achievements, the keynote was carefully crafted to connect with the thoughts and emotions of the audience, which the development team profiled very precisely. First, the developers, with a specific sense of nerdy humor and the idealism of striving to do meaningful work.

Next, the journalists, who look for reasons to question the image of the tech giant in their hunt for an attention-grabbing story.

BY UNDERSTANDING THE nuances of his audience, Sundar Pichai consistently delivered an accurate message throughout his talk. Within the first two minutes, he already drove home a clear point: Yes, we are aware of our impact on society and the responsibility that comes with it. And though we are at the forefront of technological innovation, we don't take ourselves too seriously.

Showing off the progress of the company is one goal of the keynote, of course. But another is to move the developer community to take action and build applications in the Google ecosystem. Which company would they rather be involved with: one that narrow-mindedly focuses on feature after feature? Or one that sees the full picture, delivering the framework of a meaningful company purpose while still preserving its cool? Without having to state it explicitly, the keynote's message is clear right from the beginning: Google is a fun place. Google does meaningful work. Come and join us. This is storytelling at work.

THE STYLE OF the keynote's subsequent sections was remarkable: Immediately after his opening, Pichai spoke about progress in the development of AI. Instead of showing lines of code or sharing stats on the speed and accuracy of the algorithms, he grounded the advantages of the technology in reality, putting the users and the impact of technology on their lives at the center of his narrative with descriptive stories and use cases.

How AI helps doctors in rural India make more accurate diagnoses through retina scans, for example. An emotional video showed how a disabled woman uses machine learning and morse code to communicate with her family.

Pichai's Google keynote is a storified presentation. Rather than laying on facts, it weaves those facts and data into stories, which sum up to an even bigger story: Progress is good. Technology is good. Google is good. The messages revolve around the impact of technology on people's lives rather than on the technology itself. The user stories Pichai shared express how Google technology is important because it creates value on a personal level. He wraps the clarity of a rational message in an emotional mantle and delivers it with the stickiness of a story.

WE HEAR IT over and over again: Storytelling is one of the most important tools in a leader's arsenal. But what exactly makes a story? The best way to understand is with this analogy: Ordinarily, a person is going through life in a state of equilibrium. The next moment, something happens that disturbs this order. The goal of this person, the protagonist of the story, is now to bring her world back into balance. Through action and reaction, she learns how to achieve this. The climax of the story comes when her world is stable again, but this time in a better position than before, thanks to all the learnings from along the journey.

Unlike a fact-driven presentation, which relies on data point after data point, a storifed presentation unfolds via a protagonist who is working towards some kind of change and learning by overcoming obstacles. In the course of doing so, the protagonist reveals to us, the audience, aspects of who they are.

Take Google as an example again. Instead of just stating that the company is good, the keynote showed how Google helps a disabled person live a better life through technology. This reveals the importance of inclusion and empathy as aspects of the Google brand.

The principle behind a storified presentation is that a good story delivers a message through narrated action, enabling the audience to empathize with the story's protagonist as they struggle to achieve a goal. In the process, the audience subconsciously internalizes the protagonist's actions as well as their lessons learned.

"SOMEBODY WANTS
SOMETHING BADLY AND IS HAVING
DIFFICULTY GETTING IT."
Frank Daniel

IN THE BUSINESS context, effective storytelling is about painting a picture of a desired future scenario for a customer or company. The story becomes a call to action for the audience to embrace change and collaborate towards that future: a vision packaged as a relatable narrative that enables the listener to understand what's in it for them and how they can help make it become reality.

The more vividly the story is told through examples, anecdotes, user scenarios, convincing data points, infographics, images and video content, the better its listeners will understand what actions are required, and when. And – most importantly – why it is crucial for them to take action at all. This holds true for all kinds of presentations, whether it be the pitching of a business idea, the launch of a new product, the proposal of a marketing strategy or an inspirational keynote address.

NOW, ONE COULD argue that pure facts alone should be enough to make a point. After all, we humans are rational beings. But this is only one part of the truth. As humans, we do not actually make decisions based solely on data and facts. Our decisions are heavily in-

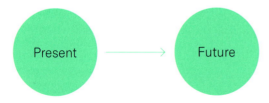

fluenced by our emotions. Psychologists are of the opinion that both aspects of our selves – the rational and the emotional – are rooted in our brains.

In his book 'The Happiness Hypothesis' psychologist Jonathan Haidt described how these two sides interact using the analogy of an elephant and its rider. The elephant represents emotions, while the rider is rationality. Because the rider sits on top of the elephant, it might appear that the rational side is in charge. But its power is limited, because compared to the elephant, the rider is relatively small. Anytime the rider and the elephant disagree, the rider will lose. The rider and the elephant, rationalism and emotion, are motivated very differently. The rider needs logical arguments – the what and the how of reaching the goal. The elephant, meanwhile, needs to hear the reasons why that goal matters in the first place.

STORIFED PRESENTATIONS SPEAK to both sides of the brain. They don't just dole out data and facts, but rather craft them into narratives relevant to the lives of the audience. Storifed presentations are essential to capturing, engaging and rewarding the audience's attention – no matter how small the meeting room or how short the presentation. Because in today's business world, all presentations are being compared to the high-end storifed presentations coming from big tech companies or given at TED events.

Getting people to listen when you speak means becoming a better storyteller, with the ability to transform data points, insights and ideas into a meaningful experience that is compelling and inspirational for your audience.

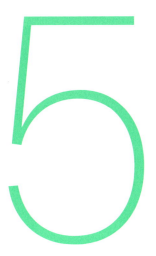

EVENTS MODELING PRESENTATION BEST PRACTICES

1

TED
-
TED is synonymous with neat, compelling and inspirational speeches.
ted.com

2

APPLE, GOOGLE & FACEBOOK
-
All three tech giants use state-of-the-art visual storytelling to present their latest products.

3

TECHCRUNCH DISRUPT
-
Based in San Francisco and one of the world's most important startup conferences with an online library of live pitches.
techcrunch.com

4

99U
-
A conference located in New York with great talks from international artists, designers and entrepreneurs.
99u.adobe.com

5

AWWWARDS CONFERENCE
-
Design professionals from Dropbox, Nike, Netflix and many more share their knowledge at this conference.
awwwards.com

SCAN THIS CODE TO GET TO THE VIDEO OF GOOGLE I/O 2018.

Susanne Klepsch, co-founder of the startup Coachfox, shares her business idea with a crowd of 250 investors in a 5-minute pitch.

ELEMENTS OF A STORY

1

PROTAGONIST

Every story needs an active protagonist. This could be the user, the company or a product. The protagonist needs to be set up in a way that the audience can relate to them (or it). This allows the listeners to project themselves into the story. Emotional stories are conveyed through the experiences of a protagonist facing major obstacles.

2

TIME & LOCATION

The time and location in which a story takes place is called the setting. It helps set up the backdrop and mood for a story. To make the setting come alive, it's important to include meaningful details. But choose those details carefully: The information should help your audience visualize the setting, but too many minor details will slow down the story rather than move it forward.

3

INCITING INCIDENT

The kickstarter of every story is the inciting incident: an event that gets the story rolling. It thrusts the protagonist into the main action of the story by creating a sort of imbalance in their life. In business, a great example of an inciting incident is the story of how Drew Houston got the inspiration for Dropbox. While on a bus trip from New York to Chicago, he realized he'd forgotten his USB drive at home, and the idea of cloud-based data storage was born.

4

GOAL

Now that the protagonist has experienced an inciting incident that brought their world out of balance, their goal is to restore that sense of order. In the life of an entrepreneur, the goal could be a vision for a product or a company. For an activist, it could be changing how society works. For a medical scientist, it could be finding a treatment for a disease.

Essential components for crafting a compelling story

FIRST ACTION

ANTAGONISTIC FORCES

ADAPTATION

CLIMAX & CLOSURE

The protagonist now takes their first action towards achieving that goal. This could be starting to work on a product, asking for advice or doing market research. The first action is the most obvious step the protagonist can take to get closer to their goal. But rarely does it lead to instant results.

The story begins to get interesting when the protagonist doesn't get what they want right away. Conflict with antagonistic forces creates tension. Remember Frank Daniel's definition of a story: "Somebody wants something badly and is having difficulty getting it." There are different kinds of forces: the protagonist's surroundings (nature, society, a system), another person, time, and physiological or psychological constraints, just to mention a few.

The antagonistic forces compel the protagonist to adapt strategies to get closer to their goal. To get further, they need to find a creative solution. The decisions the protagonist makes along the way reveal their character. We as an audience can only understand the logic behind a solution if we also understood the logic of the problem it solves. These moments of adaptation to antagonistic forces repeat until the moment the solution is found.

The climax of the story comes when the protagonist reaches their goal. It is often the most exciting part of the story: when the hero saves the princess or discovers the buried treasure. The entrepreneur finally develops their product, the activist changes society for the better and the scientist develops the cure for a disease. The world's balance is restored and everyone benefits from the adventurous journey of the protagonist.

THE HERO'S JOURNEY
A blueprint for stories that resonate

THE HERO'S JOURNEY is one of the most important narrative principles behind great stories. Many popular Hollywood movies, from Star Wars to Inception, follow its logic. The Hero's Journey is about a protagonist who goes on an adventure, wins a decisive victory after a crisis, and returns home transformed. Understanding the narrative principles of the Hero's Journey can help anyone tell better stories.

The Hero's Journey was first explored by Joseph Campbell back in the 1940s. As a researcher of comparative mythology, Campbell analyzed the mythological tales of indigenous peoples all across the globe. He searched for insights on how storytelling was used by myriad cultures to share knowledge and experiences with one another. While trying to understand what made these stories such effective communication tools, he discovered a pattern: The same types of characters appeared again and again, and all the stories followed the same 17 stages. He named this pattern the monomyth.

DECADES LATER, SCREENWRITER and story consultant Christopher Vogler adapted the Hero's Journey for the movie industry in Los Angeles, condensing the pattern to 12 stages. Since then, the narrative framework of the Hero's Journey has been adapted by the advertising industry to create story-like campaigns for brands like Apple (e.g. the Macbook Air campaign) and Nike (e.g. the Find Your Greatness campaign).

In parallel, the insights also found their way to another campfire of modern society: the stage of the TED conference. As a metaphor, the hero in a TED talk could be anyone: a scientist who finally makes a groundbreaking discovery after years of research and setbacks. An artist who works to help society gain a deeper understanding of human nature. An entrepreneur who builds a product to turn sewage into drinking water.

OR AN ATHLETE who challenges society's definition of beauty. Like Aimee Mullins, who was born without fibular bones and has walked on prosthetic legs since childhood. Later in life, Mullins became a champion sprinter, setting world records at the 1996 Paralympics in Atlanta. She also became a model and actress, walking in a runway show for Alexander McQueen and appearing as the Leopard Queen in Matthew Barney's Cremaster Cycle. Her mission became to change society's perception of prosthetics. In her TED talk "My 12 Pairs of Legs" she showed her prosthetics, from purely functional ones to real works of art.

But even more moving were her reflections on how her conversation with society as a person wearing prosthetics has changed, from a conversation about overcoming disability to a conversation about augmentation. A quintessential Hero's Journey which made her a great role model for the TED audience.

SCAN THIS CODE TO GET TO AIMEE'S TED TALK.

Storytelling 033

10
Aimee brings all her legs back home to Manhattan and goes to a party.
-
The hero takes the road back and recommits to completing the journey.

11
A lady who Aimee meets at the party says it's not fair Aimee can make herself so tall by wearing prosthetic legs.
-
The climax in which the hero must have her final encounter with death.

12
Aimee's conversation with society about prosthetics has changed – from overcoming deficiencies to augmentation.
-
The hero returns with the elixir to benefit the ordinary world.

→ **1**
Adults are uncertain about how to react when Aimee brings a selection of her prosthetic legs to an event at a school.
-
The audience meets the hero in the ordinary world.

2
A kid playing around with Aimee's prosthetics asks, "Hey, why wouldn't you wanna fly too?"
-
The hero receives the call to adventure, a challenge, quest or a problem that must be faced.

3
Aimee doesn't really hesitate. She's a very proactive character.
-
The hero expresses fear and is reluctant or refuses the call.

9
After years of experimentation Aimee now owns 12 pairs of legs with completely different features.
-
The hero has cheated death and is rewarded. The much-sought-after prize is hers.

8
In collaboration with the artist Matthew Barney, Aimee discovers that her legs can be wearable sculpture.
-
The hero endures the ordeal, the central crisis in which she confronts her biggest fear and tastes death.

7
Aimee walks the runway for Alexander McQueen on a pair of wooden legs.
-
The hero makes their final preparations and approaches the inmost cave.

6
Aimee has conversations with people about the definition of disability.
-
The hero learns about the special world through tests, encountering allies and enemies.

5
Aimee's call to innovators to help her envision and build new prosthetic legs.
-
The hero finally accepts the challenge and crosses the threshold into the special world.

4
The 8-year-old not only verbalizes Aimee's call to adventure but also becomes her mentor by enabling her to see potential she wasn't aware of.
-
A meeting with the mentor provides confidence, wisdom or magical gifts to push the hero beyond fear.

Beyond The Obvious

THREE-ACT STRUCTURE
The backbone of a story

OPENING BEAT
Every presentation should have a strong beginning – this is how you catch the attention of the audience right away. Examples of an opening beat could be an anecdote, an impressive fact or some kind of interaction with the audience. What's important is that it drives the story instantly.

TRANSITION – HOOK
A transition keeps the story floating from the first act into the second. This could be a guiding question or the stating of a protagonist's goal. Sometimes, the transition can be an abrupt switch after a personal anecdote, like a second beginning to the presentation. From this point, the rest of the story unfolds.

ACT 1 – SETTING THE SCENE
Establish the general background against which a story takes place: the location, time period and protagonist. Answer the Five W Questions: who, what, where, when and why.

ACT 2 – IMMERSION
The middle act of the presentation is the longest of all three. In this part, all aspects of the overall topic are described more in depth. To help orient the audience, the central act should be divided into chapters.

Agile Presentation Design

LIKE EVERYTHING IN life, each story has a beginning, a middle and an end. This basic structure just "feels right" for the audience and works for stories as short as three sentences as well as presentations of three hours. Subdividing into three acts provides a basic framework for organizing your content in an impactful way.

CLOSING BEAT

Just as your presentation started with a clear beginning, it should also end with one. This is called the closing beat. According to the peak-end rule, people most clearly remember the most emotional moment and the end of an experience. Think of a way to anchor your content in the audience's minds. If you tie it back to your opening, this is called a closed story form.

TRANSITION – WRAP-UP

Act 2 and Act 3 are again connected with a transition. In many talks, this transition is a brief summary of the content that has come before.

MINI-TRANSITIONS

All chapters are linked through mini-transitions.

CHAPTERS

Just like in a book or long article, a presentation can be broken down into chapters to provide guidance and orientation. Each chapter provides the answer to a sub-question of the presentation's overarching theme. The chapters are built as mini-stories with a clear beginning, middle and end.

ACT 3 – CONCLUSION

The last act provides the space to wrap up the presentation and set its messages into perspective. This can take the form of a request, a prolonged version of a call to action, or a moral or personal positioning.

"The most powerful person in the world is the storyteller."

Steve Jobs

Expert Interview   The Explorer
                          ‾‾‾‾‾‾‾‾‾‾‾‾

Design Thinking is one of the best methodologies for finding innovative solutions to real-world problems. The process, developed over decades in the ecosystem of Stanford University, is used by companies like Airbnb, Dropbox and Google to develop new products, services and strategies. It begins with gaining as much empathy for the user as possible: the groundwork for any great design. Once the user and their needs have been defined, quick prototypes are produced and tested directly in the hands of the user. The next step is integrating the user's feedback into the next iteration of the prototype. This process is repeated until the product is finished. Involving the end user right away and working co-creatively with them throughout the design process ensures the final result really meets their needs. I combine design thinking with storytelling to produce more convincing visual stories. For me, the audience is the user and the presentation is the product. Turning data points into inspiring stories – iteration over iteration.

    Carissa Carter is the Head of Teaching and Learning at the d.school at Stanford University. I interviewed Carter to get her insights on design thinking, the creative process and the role of communication in innovation.

CARISSA, WHY DOES THE WORLD NEED A DESIGN MINDSET?
We have so many interesting challenges in the world right now, whether it's around providing access to clean energy for everybody, connecting devices at home or educating our children, and we need design to help us tackle all these topics. Design can help us get more human about what we are creating. It can help us be more aware of the people that are in our ecosystem and it can also help us quickly scale and try out new ideas and new problem spaces and test the limits of the businesses that we already have.

HOW WOULD YOU DESCRIBE THE IMPORTANCE OF A DESIGN MINDSET IN BUSINESS?
Design can help you find new ideas for what to work on. If you want to create a new product, a new experience or a new system in the world, we have today the tools and techniques to make absolutely anything, and it's design that helps you actually make that happen. I mean, we can always get better. Design and business have historically worked well together.

YOU ONCE SAID THAT FOLLOWING THE DESIGN THINKING PROCESS IS LIKE LEARNING TO COOK. COULD YOU ELABORATE A BIT ON THAT?
When I say "the process," I am referring to a diagram of hexagons that is basically five different steps. And that's a very common way to introduce new people to design. Sometimes it's hexagons, sometimes you might see a double-diamond in-out converge-diverge – there are a few different versions of that design process diagram. When learning the process, the diagram is great because when you are learning to cook, you follow a recipe. The very first time you do a design project it's also nice to follow a recipe, because you get to a result that you feel – hopefully – pretty good about in the end, and you get a sense for what the different modes feel like. But as you get better, just like with cooking, you start swapping a few ingredients. And then when you get really good you can work with the constraints you have. Like, you have orange juice and broccoli in the fridge – what can you do with that in 10 minutes' time? And in that moment you can begin to call yourself a chef. Although I don't know if a chef would make anything from those ingredients… but you know what I mean. And it's the same with design.

IN ADDITION TO THE DESIGN THINKING PROCESS, WHAT ARE THE DESIGN FACULTIES YOU TEACH AT STANFORD?
At d.school, if you peel back all the different processes that we might teach students in classes, at the core of it are the eight different design abilities. They are the things we are aiming to enable in our students. They include being able

Design Thinking

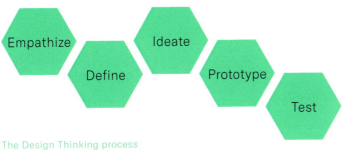

The Design Thinking process as taught at d.school at Stanford University, California

FACTS WORTH KNOWING ABOUT DESIGN THINKING

1

THE BUSINESS IMPACT
-
In 2018, IBM conducted a study on the business impact a design mindset has on a company. Project teams reduced development and testing time by 33%, helped projects cut design defects by 50% and overall helped cut project costs significantly.

2

THE INGREDIENTS
-
Team, process, room. For a successful Design Thinking project, it's very important to choose a diverse and complementary team, to have a room set up for creative thinking and to be mindful about the process the team will be going through.

3

THE TOOLS
-
Post-it notes and a marker are by far the most common and useful tools for getting ideas out of the head into the world.

to learn from other people in other contexts, being able to rapidly experiment, and make things fast. Whether that's ideas you are moving around or rough prototypes, they are about building and crafting intentionally. We also teach about synthesizing information, so bringing together both quantitative and qualitative information, finding patterns, seeing insights, finding things that other people aren't noticing. Those are four tangible things we teach.

Then we also have four intangible abilities: One is to be able to move from the concrete to the abstract, so it's almost to be able to zoom in and out of a problem. Another is to be able to design your design work. So, to know and be able to have that plan and know the right tools for the task, to be able to communicate deliberately, so whether you are talking to a room full of 200 people and pitching an idea or you need to debrief with a project partner after a project and reflect on what happened, you need to have tools to do that. And finally, one that I think is the most important right now, is to be able to navigate ambiguity. And when I say ambiguity, I mean all of that uncertainty that's in the world right now.

WHY IS COMMUNICATION SO IMPORTANT IN THE INNOVATION PROCESS?
We are thinking about communication throughout. Whether you are just starting an innovation project and you need to figure out what to create, you are communicating with many of those different stakeholders that are part of your project. And whether that's a potential end user or somebody that might be a distributor of the product you have in the end – you want to understand their needs and look for the right opportunity. So that's communication that happens early on as you are figuring out what to make. But then there is also the communication as you are working with your team to build and create. How are we making sure we're using the skills that you're really strong in and parallel-ing that with the ones I am strong in; how are we being aware not to pull somebody else in, and then to whom and how are we communicating about what we've created?

THANK YOU VERY MUCH, CARISSA!

Visual thinking is one of the core activities in the creative process, as it brings ideas to life immediately.

THE KNOWLEDGE FUNNEL

1

MYSTERY STAGE
-
A design process starts with many uncertainties. At the beginning it's difficult to explain the idea or concept, as there are infinite options for how to tell the story. No clear path is visible.

2

HEURISTIC STAGE
-
In the next stage, a clearer understanding of the content is developed. Think "rule of thumb." The knowledge becomes more manageable. First documents are produced. We use storyboards and text to organize our thinking. The storyboards help us to evaluate the narrative structure and see the bigger picture of our story. The text forces us to boil down our thoughts into accurate words and sentences.

Creative Process 045

Transforming vague ideas into solid concepts

THE DESIGN THINKING mindset of rapid prototyping, testing and iteration helps create much more concise and targeted presentations. Generally speaking, every presentation design process is a process of acquiring new knowledge and gaining a deeper understanding of a topic. Through developing the presentation (form), the author will also further develop the original idea (content). As a model, the Knowledge Funnel developed by Canadian management professor Roger Martin helps anyone who is crafting a new presentation, concept or business model to understand where they are in the thinking and editing process.

3

ALGORITHM STAGE
-
Through intensive thinking, the content has been converted from a vague idea into a solid concept with a coherent story. The author now knows exactly what message they want to convey. For a presentation, this means a script has been written. Every word should be precisely the right word, at the right place. The presentation slides have been designed simply and accurately, and synchronize with the script. The presentation handout is a combined version of the slide deck and the text. All professional presentations have reached this stage.

THERE WILL BE DRAGONS

The struggles of the creative process, why it's so difficult to get your ideas to the point and how to get it done anyway

ANALYSIS PARALYSIS

Problem
-
Often, people approach presentation development in an overly rational way. The desire to create a perfect final product often keeps people from getting started at all. This phenomenon is called Analysis Paralysis: every piece of information seems equally important and worthy of inclusion. We tell ourselves we must work through each and every bit of content before we can begin sharing it with others.

Solution
-
Don't overthink it – just start by getting something down on the page. Set yourself a time limit and make an initial rough draft within this deadline. As writer Jodi Picoult puts it: "You can always edit a bad page. But you can't edit a blank page."

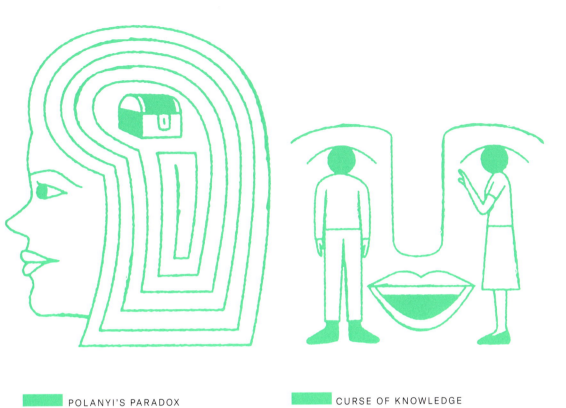

POLANYI'S PARADOX

Problem
-
The challenge in designing a presentation is to formulate implicit or tacit knowledge in an explicit way. It's as if there is knowledge within us that we don't have complete, conscious access to. This effect is called Polanyi's Paradox – we know more than we are capable of expressing.

Solution
-
Present drafts of your presentation to others, even early on, in order to collect feedback on how well your ideas are coming across. Explaining ideas to others and answering their questions is a good way to ascertain the most important aspects of a topic. Often, we'll arrive at explanations we would not have come up with on our own.

CURSE OF KNOWLEDGE

Problem
-
The so-called Curse of Knowledge is the bias that results when we have mastered an area of information so well that we can't put ourselves in the shoes of someone who doesn't possess that same understanding. Though our insights and their meanings are crystal clear in our minds, we cannot communicate them to others – a phenomenon evident in experts in every kind of field.

Solution
-
Work to develop as much empathy for your audience as possible. To communicate effectively, you must first understand exactly who your listeners are, what they already know and what objectives they have.

IDEAS HAVE THEIR OWN LIFE

Problem
-
Ideas are like pubescent teenagers: moody and subject to their own whims. Though we can't control exactly when a great idea will strike, we can create the best possible conditions to facilitate them.

Solution
-
Immerse yourself in the ins and outs of your topic and build up your presentation's content. Then step away from your work and let your thoughts wander. Take a walk, daydream, maybe do some exercise. When the brain is in relaxation mode, it develops new ways of connecting the information already drifting around in there. Insights and eureka moments often strike when we're not actively seeking them.

CHAOTIC VS. LINEAR

Problem
-
Working creatively is often an associative process, meaning that one idea leads us to another. A presentation, on the other hand, is a linear communication process, with one person speaking to a group of others. Creating a presentation means deciding which information will be shared, and in what linear order.

Solution
-
A tried-and-tested way to find the right presentation structure is to borrow one from a story. One shortcut would be setting a creative limit in the form of a list structure, such as "The five most important things we learned with our project." Define what these five points are, and you've already got the outline for your presentation.

The creative process

Public speaking is public thinking.

CREATIVE THINKING MODES

1 THINKING

Thinking is important, but in its basic form, it can be a pretty shallow activity. We may have moments of clear insights and epiphany, but these are so easily disturbed by internal impulses (thinking about what to watch on Netflix tonight) as well as external impulses (our smartphone). To achieve in-depth insights, we need to supplement with other modes of thinking.

2 SPEAKING THINKING

Finding the right words for ideas and thoughts and speaking them out loud is the first crucial step when starting work on a presentation or concept. As the German philosopher Heinrich von Kleist once wrote: "Speech is nothing other than thinking aloud. The succession of ideas and the expression of those ideas proceed side by side, and the mental processes of the two converge."

3 BODY THINKING

Body language is the translation of mental images into physical actions. Therefore, the ability to express a thought through movement is a great indicator of whether one's thinking has been honed as sharply as it can. If you are struggling to express concepts with gestures, you may need to spend some more time boiling down your thoughts into graspable images and metaphors.

4 VISUAL THINKING

Ever since our Paleolithic ancestors were drawing on the walls of their caves, humans have been developing their thinking through visual means. As the visual thinking legend Robert H. McKim once put it: "Drawing helps you to bring vague inner images into focus." When crafting your presentation, pen and paper should become your best friends. Before touching your computer for the first time, create a storyboard of your presentation's outline on paper.

Great presentations are based on deliberate, in-depth thinking

WRITING THINKING

BREAKS

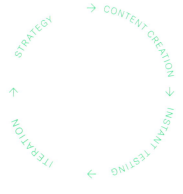

PRESENTATION DESIGN
=
PRODUCT DESIGN

To really crystallize your thinking, write down the complete concept of your presentation, in complete sentences. Doing so requires re-thinking your ideas with greater clarity. This step is not about creating a script to be memorized and repeated in front of your audience. It's about the process of writing itself!

Just as our muscles need rest between workouts to grow strong, our minds need breaks between creative sessions to further develop an idea or concept. Ideas often emerge when our brain is in relaxation mode, and during sleep is when the brain consolidates new learning. As researchers at the University of Lübeck discovered, "sleeping on a problem" can improve our ability to recognize patterns in data sets by up to 40%.

DEVELOPING A CRISP presentation follows the same principles as agile product design. In my work with startups in various accelerator programs, I first help the teams clarify the context of their pitch presentation, their objective and their target audience in particular. Afterwards, they create a first rapid prototype of their pitch in the form of a storyboard, a simple visualization of all aspects of their business idea sketched out on Post-it notes and put into sequence. With this exercise, the teams are already generating a shared understanding of what they want to present to their potential investors. The next step is to present those ideas to an audience in public pitch training sessions to generate feedback. I advise the teams to harvest the comments and questions they receive and integrate the answers into the next iteration of their presentation.

Printing out the slides of a presentation is helpful for checking the coherence of the story arc and the visual design.

THE FOUR FORMATS

1

One-liner

A one-liner is the most distilled, pared-down summary of what your presentation is about. The goal of the one-liner is to make your idea graspable in just one sentence. It should be written in a manner that even people who know nothing about your presentation or topic get its meaning right away. It might cross-connect to the core message of your presentation or your mission statement. Though there is no standardized format, a good template to start with is the following: [Name of your idea] + [customer-related verb] + [customer segment] + [job to be done] + [service or product].
Here is an example: Foodscovery [name] is a global marketplace [service] that connects [customer-related verb] producers of authentic local food to foodies [customer segment] all over the world.
The template functions like a springboard into your first draft. It will take some iterations until you have the perfect sentence.

2

Elevator Pitch

The elevator pitch lasts for up to 90 seconds and explains your idea on a deeper level than the one-liner. It is a very useful tool to have in your arsenal at networking events, in interviews or even on stage. The goal of the elevator pitch is to get a potential investor interested in further discussions. The information you share in this pitch should be reduced to the absolute, most relevant essentials. You could open with your one-liner, then move from there to the big picture and problem statement, followed by a brief product demo. To highlight the scope of the investment opportunity you could mention market size and your USP, your team and what your next steps are. At the end, you should have a clear call to action that needs to be catered to your specific target group. Though you only have 90 seconds, you should never feel rushed while presenting your elevator pitch, so make sure the content is edited down to fit the time limit.

From one sentence to a full conference keynote

3

Business Pitch

A good business pitch weaves all business-relevant components into a unique storyline. It usually lasts 5–10 minutes and explains the business idea more in-depth. This is the standard pitch format used by startups all over the world. It can be used on stage, and also as a meeting opener to get everyone on the same page. The goal of the business pitch is to get your idea across and – as with the elevator pitch – hook a potential investor into further discussions. Even in as little as 5 minutes, you can persuasively sum up the most important components of your business idea, like the problem, your solution and product vision, market-relevant figures, and operational information like your roadmap. Be sure not to jump from one component to another. Look for a storyline that connects all the parts in a cohesive narrative. For a look at my business pitch storyboard, turn to page 112.

4

Keynote

A keynote presentation usually takes 10–45 minutes. Longer product keynotes can take up to 2 hours, but are divided into various speakers. In that case, I suggest going for 10–15 minutes maximum per speech. A presentation can be educational, informative or entertaining – or in the best-case scenario, all three. Keynotes on conference stages are a great format to build a personal brand and reach opinion leaders. Internal keynotes are great opportunities to demonstrate leadership, providing employees with guidance and instilling confidence in the management team. As the widespread popularity of the TED-style talk has shown, it's clear that a keynote should be told as a story. Unlike a business pitch, which has very clearly predefined narrative components, a keynote allows much more freedom, though with this freedom comes more complexity. Getting a keynote to a professional level can easily take 80–90 hours of work.

THE FIVE DELIVERABLES

1
Outline

2
Script

WHEN YOU'RE AT the starting line of designing a presentation, keep in mind the 5 components, or deliverables, you'll need to produce along the way. All 5 of these apply to both the business pitch and the inspirational keynote. Each serves a specific purpose and cannot be replaced by one of the other components. Start by building a rough version of all of them right at the start of the design process, developing and polishing them as you go along – right up until the day of the presentation.

The outline lays out the concept of the keynote from an outside descriptive perspective. It covers the overall idea and the structure of the presentation.

Every word the speaker plans to say at any given point in the presentation needs to be precisely written out. Not to be memorized by heart, but to be carefully thought through.

Deliverables 059

Essential documents of a professional presentation

3
Storyboard

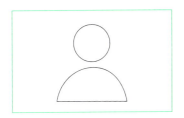

The storyboard is a graphic framework consisting of the presentation's written message and corresponding visual translations. The storyboard begins as a series of simple sketches, which gradually evolve into the final slides.

4
Slides

The slides are the visual aids to a presentation. Each slide should convey just one message. Keeping the slides as simple as possible ensures the audience will stay focused on the speaker.

5
Handout

The handout is the self-explanatory version of a presentation. It combines the visuals used on the slides with text from the script, adapted in style for readability.

Outro

Storytelling and design thinking will help you to craft better presentations. Once you understand the architecture of great stories and the inner workings of the creative process you know that a great presentation is all about in-depth thinking. To become a better storyteller, there are four areas in which you can improve your skills. 1st – Strategy: Clarifying the context and knowing your goals are key to targeted communication. 2nd – Story: It's simple – the better you know how stories work, the better you can tell them. 3rd – Visuals: Becoming better in UX/UI design helps to design more effective slides. 4th – Delivery: Great speakers know how to engage an audience. All four skills can be learned and practiced. Becoming better in one field will make you a better storyteller overall.

Can't get enough?

Books

THE WRITER'S JOURNEY
Christopher Vogler. A classic for screenwriters, writers and anyone who wants to understand the art of storytelling.

THE DESIGN OF BUSINESS
Roger Martin. A fundamental book about design thinking including the theory of the knowledge funnel.

Links

ALFRED STARTUP PITCH
CEO Marcela Sapone presents her business at TechCrunch Disrupt.
youtube.com/watch?v=xYKt5YgVOpk

THE RAPID GROWTH OF THE CHINESE INTERNET
This talk pushes storytelling to the next level. ted.com/garyliu

ON STORYTELLING
Famed radio host Ira Glass reveals some secrets of his craft.
thisamericanlife.org/extras/ira-glass-on-storytelling

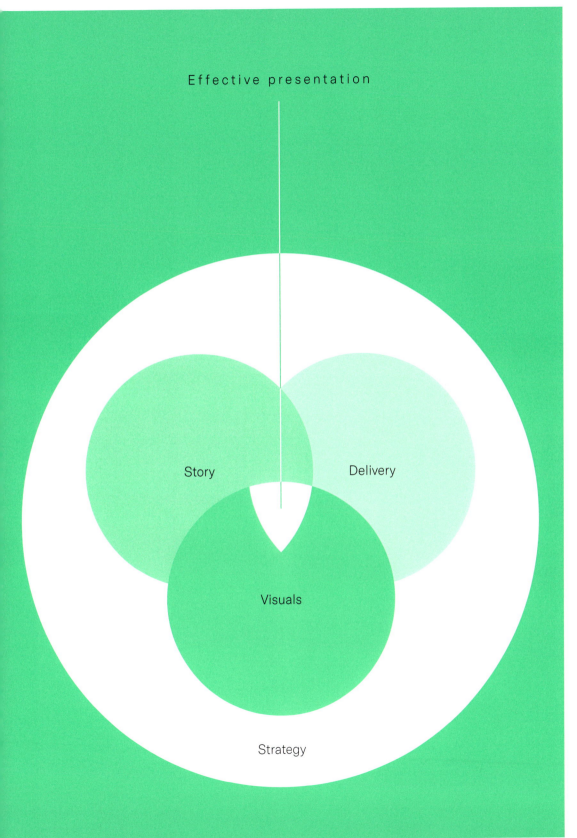

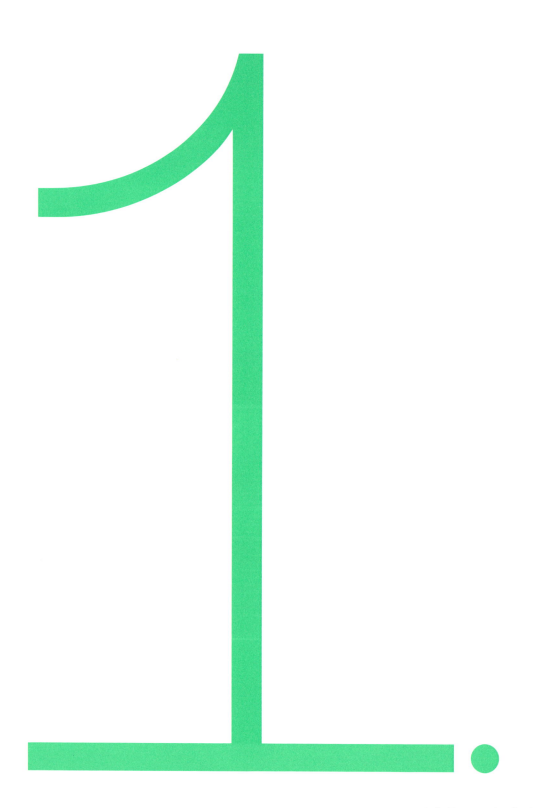

Agile Presentation Design

Chapter One   Define

Even if it may feel counterintuitive, before starting to work on the content of your presentation, you first need to take a step back. Evaluate and define the context and the core message you want to convey. This step is crucial to creating a coherent, comprehensive presentation more efficiently. The first step in presentation design is crafting your communication strategy. You need to develop an in-depth understanding of your "why" – the specific goal of your presentation – and also gain as much empathy for your audience as possible. This means understanding how they can benefit from your ideas and information, as well as predicting their potential counter-arguments. This is the best way to target your messages precisely to your listeners' needs. Based on this preparation, you can now start mapping out your content, defining your future scenario and distilling your core message.

Sound like a lot? Not to worry – I'll get you there!

1	2	3	4	5
- Strategy	- Mind Map	- Polar Opposites	- Future Scenario	- Core Message
p. 74	p. 82	p. 84	p. 86	p. 90

"Great stories happen to those who can tell them."

Ira Glass

Expert Interview   The Explainer

All innovation begins with the exploration of the unknown – looking for patterns and drawing connections between seemingly disparate ideas. It's a process that requires collaboration, and the capability to distill complex ideas into simple, powerful stories that ignite action. And who would know better about the effectiveness of good storytelling than journalists? Their job is to classify and arrange the complexity of the world's events into meaningful narratives. Journalists are practiced in spotting a potential story and unearthing it through accurate observation and systematic research. Like a good presentation, a strong piece of journalism is a depictive story that helps its readers digest data while resonating with them on a deeper emotional level.

    Nearly a decade, Thomas Schulz worked as a business correspondent in the U.S. for the German news magazine Der SPIEGEL. Based in San Francisco, he covered Silicon Valley and the tech industry. His long-form reporting focuses on analyzing leading internet and high-tech companies, taking deep-dives into the technological progress driving computer science and biotech. For years, Thomas has been writing about the impact of the digital revolution on society, politics and culture. I spoke with him about the underlying principles of his craft, his unique creative process and how he brings ideas to life.

WHAT GOOGLE REALLY WANTS
-
Thomas's first bestselling book explained the objectives of the tech giant. It has been translated into 15 languages.

THOMAS, WHAT ARE THE COMPONENTS OF A GOOD STORY FOR YOU?
People. Always! And examples. Anecdotes, definitely. And putting it all together with structure – the story definitely should not be all over the place. Having these elements all separate from one another doesn't work. Nor does stringing them together randomly. And through it all, you have to show that you really understand your material. You have to demonstrate to your reader that you've got it through and through. If that isn't clear at the very beginning, you've already lost credibility from the start.

HOW DO YOU FIND THE STORIES YOU WANT TO TELL?
In my experience, the stories I personally find exciting are also the stories that other people find interesting. It's totally inconsequential whether you're a specialist or a complete amateur. What you need to ask yourself with any story is this: What is the truly exciting thing about this? It can even be something totally banal. The task, then, is to convey that moment of excitement. The simple and banal hooks everyone. From there I get into the detail, otherwise you can lose many readers just in the first five sentences.

CURIOSITY LEADS YOU TO THE THINGS YOU FIND EXCITING – THEN WHAT COMES NEXT?
Next comes diving into the material – research, doing interviews and collecting examples of whether the story is really as interesting as originally thought. That curiosity needs to be backed up with a truly good story.

HOW DO YOU DEFINE YOUR AUDIENCE, AND HOW DO YOU GET INSIGHTS INTO YOUR READERS?
The first thing is to look at what medium you're serving. Only then can you define your audience. Then I naturally have the problem that my audience is so big that I can only work in broad, generalized groupings. So I come at it from the other side. Not: Who is my audience? But rather: What interests all people?

A STORY WILL INSPIRE DIFFERENT IMAGES IN EVERY READER'S HEAD. IS THIS SOMETHING YOU KEEP IN MIND WHILE WRITING?
That's a question you always have to ask yourself, of course. But there are many variances – depending on whether you're telling a completely new story, or approaching a well-known one from a new perspective. An old story that people already know has to be told in an exciting way to present new facets. If you're telling of something the reader has never known before, you have to start from the very beginning. That demands an entirely different thought process.

"PEOPLE. ALWAYS! AND EXAMPLES. ANECDOTES, DEFINITELY. AND PUTTING IT ALL TOGETHER WITH STRUCTURE – THE STORY SHOULD NOT BE ALL OVER THE PLACE. HAVING THESE ELEMENTS ALL SEPARATE FROM ONE ANOTHER DOESN'T WORK."

Agile Presentation Design

HOW DO YOU FIND THE ENTRY POINT INTO YOUR STORIES?

That totally depends on what kind of story I'm writing. If I want to tell an entertaining story that's filled with anecdotes, then of course I open with these entertaining anecdotes. If I am beginning a story on an extremely complicated topic, then I will open with an explanatory anecdote or two very simple sentences that get right to the heart of the topic. For this reason, the opening is often the most difficult part. There's that famous Henri Nannen quote: "Begin with an earthquake and build up slowly from there." You need to have that in your head. Begin with clear language. It's very important to hook people in with a strong opening. There are so many different options. The opening can be anecdotal, or empathic, or it can also be a provocative or surprising statement.

MOVING ON FROM THE BEGINNING TO THE ENDING – HOW IMPORTANT IS THE END OF A STORY?

You definitely should not be fading away at the end. Everyone is naturally going to remember the last thing they read or heard. You can write 350 exciting pages, but if the last few are blah, that's what people will remember. If you're opening with an earthquake, you shouldn't be closing with a ripple. Pick up the momentum again at the end.

HOW CAN YOU TELL WHEN YOU'VE TRULY GRASPED THE TOPIC?

I get a sense for it when I'm writing it down. When I notice that I'm not able to tell a story, it's always because I don't know what I should be telling. And not knowing what I should tell is always due to not fully understanding the material. When I'm at this point where I'm having to deliberate things too much, it's time to collect more information: research, do interviews, rework things. It's always the same process.

HOW DO YOU SORT INFORMATION?

I have to be structured, or else I'll go under. Part of my structuring process is identifying individual themes and categorizing all the information under these themes. Because if I structure the information incorrectly, then I won't be able to communicate it meaningfully to others.

AT WHICH POINT DO YOU LET OTHERS BE PART OF YOUR WRITING PROCESS?

Right from the beginning. I always let people read the introduction, in order to see whether the topic and the entry point work and are interesting to others. If people already respond at this point with "No" or "What's this about," or "I don't get it – boring," then I know I have reworking to do.

THANK YOU VERY MUCH, THOMAS!

THE FUTURE OF MEDICINE
-
Thomas's second book, published in 2018, was an immediate bestseller, telling the story of how technology and medicine are merging.

Effective communication is receiver-oriented.

Presentation Strategy

1.1

1

WHY

When crafting a speech, the first step is to ask yourself why you're giving this presentation: What's your motivation? It can come down to personal or career reasons, such as wanting to drive a particular project forward. Only once you've worked out the "why" can you stand before your audience with drive and all the right arguments to back up your idea. Presentations without a "why" are vague and unfocused. The more concretely you formulate yours, the better!

2

WHO

Next, turn your focus on your audience: Listener-oriented communication relies on knowing exactly who you're talking to. If your audience is large and diverse, get a clearer overview by dividing the group into segments. Think closely about all the people who will be in the audience when you present, but also those who will come into contact with your content at a later time. Prioritize the various target groups.

Agile Presentation Design

The foundation of effective storytelling

3
AUDIENCE PROFILE

Now that you've got an overview of who you'll be presenting to, it's time to work out which audience members or target groups are of particular importance for you. An audience profile creates a clear picture of these listeners and also helps you develop empathy. What are the character traits of this audience, where do they stand on your topic and what are their expectations of you? The more you know about your listeners, the better you can tailor your content precisely to them.

4
BENEFITS

For your audience, what matters is that they can benefit in some way from your presentation and its content. When you take the stage and begin to speak, every listener is subconsciously asking themselves, "What's in this for me?" So be sure to ask yourself: "Which audience needs can my presentation fulfill? To what extent can I ensure they'll walk away with the concrete ability to do something better, faster, more efficiently or with more enjoyment than before?"

5
COUNTER-ARGUMENTS

Compile all possible counter-arguments that could weaken your position. Addressing these within your presentation prevents your audience from getting distracted. Otherwise, they will be mentally pondering the counter-arguments themselves and no longer listening to you. What's more, addressing counter-arguments enables you to proactively frame your content rather than letting the audience hijack aspects of your idea.

6
SMART GOAL

What is the specific, concrete goal you want to achieve with your presentation? Take the time to define your SMART goal (smart, measurable, appropriate, realistic and time bound). In the startup context, a SMART goal could be generating funding. E.g.: Our goal is to raise €300,000 to move our idea into the project phase, to hire at least three people with a background in UX design, tech and business development, and to have the prototype ready by the end of the year.

COMMUNICATION STYLES
How people get their message across

COMMUNICATING EFFECTIVELY IS about matching your own communication style to that of your listeners. For this reason, gaining empathy for your audience should not only include understanding the broader context like your audience's background, expectations, values and interests, but also understanding how they prefer to communicate. Adapting to their communication style will improve their receptiveness to what you have to say.

There are four basic types of communication styles:

ADAPTED FROM ROBERT YOUKER, PROJECT MANAGEMENT WORLD JOURNAL

1
ACTION-ORIENTED
-
Keep it short and simple. Action-oriented people like the feeling of getting things done, so focus on objectives and results when presenting to them. People with this style do not appreciate being given too many alternatives – they want to hear the few best recommendations as briefly as possible. The practicality of an idea should be highlighted. The "what" of an idea should be in the foreground. Help an action-oriented person with strong visual aids.

2
IDEA-ORIENTED
-
Being very curious minds, the "why" behind a concept is important to an idea-oriented person. Open by emphasizing how your topic is connected to a bigger picture or idea. Point out the uniqueness and the innovative potential of your idea and emphasize its potential future value. Idea-oriented people love to seek possibilities and opportunities and the grandest possible design.

3
PEOPLE-ORIENTED
-
"What is the effect on other people?" is a classic question from people with this communication style. They look for the "who" in an idea, so always show the impact on relevant stakeholders. Indicate how the idea has already worked well in the past, and mention the project's support from well-respected people. In terms of language, use colloquial language or an informal writing style, as this is often how members of people-related organizations like human resources tend to communicate.

4
PROCESS-ORIENTED
-
The process-oriented person seeks details and facts, so be very precise when communicating to her, structuring your presentation step by step. They want to understand how a specific idea can be implemented. As people with this style like to understand the matter to the greatest level of detail, offer them options including the potential advantages and disadvantages of an idea. Also: Do not rush a process-oriented person.

Strategy 075

Presentation Strategy Worksheet

This form helps you to clarify the context of your presentation and define your communication goal.

1 Why? What are your personal and professional key drivers for this presentation?

2 Who? Who will be the receivers of your presentation? Do you know their names, or can you cluster them into segments?

_____
_____
_____
_____
_____

_____
_____
_____
_____
_____

3 Audience Profile

NAME
GENDER / AGE
JOB TITLE
LOCATION
BACKGROUND

DEPTH OF KNOWLEDGE
OBJECTIVES
EXPECTATIONS
VALUES
INTERESTS / LIFESTYLE
SELF-PERCEPTION
SOCIAL PERCEPTION
TYPICAL QUOTE
COMMUNICATION STYLE

4 Benefits

How do they benefit from your idea?

5 Counter-arguments

What could your audience potentially ask that might weaken your position? What would your answer be?

COUNTER-ARGUMENT
YOUR ANSWER

6 SMART Goal

E.g.: Our goal is to raise €300,000 to move our idea into the project phase, to hire at least three people with a background in UX design, tech and business development, and to have the prototype ready by the end of the year.

_____
_____
_____

Beyond The Obvious

Creating an effective presentation requires accurate strategic planning in advance.

SCAN THIS CODE TO GET TO FABIAN'S TED TALK.

Agile Presentation Design

The Shaper

When Fabian Hemmert walked onto the stage of the TEDxBerlin conference in 2009, he could not have imagined the tremendous journey that was lying ahead. A young design researcher at the time in the Design Research Lab at the Berlin University of the Arts, Hemmert was at TEDxBerlin to give the audience a glimpse into his work at the institute. He gave the audience a thrilling demo of the potential future of the mobile phone: three prototypes of shape-shifting and weight-shifting handhelds that also showed off the breadth of his creative potential. Later, the editors at TED chose his talk for uploading onto the official TED.com site. Since then, his talk has been watched more than 900,000 times and translated into over 35 languages, and Hemmert has been invited to speak at numerous events all around the globe.

Today, he is a Professor for Interface and User Experience Design at the University of Wuppertal. Fabian Hemmert loves more than just design: He is also passionate about interpersonal communication and public speaking. To prepare for his five minutes on stage at TEDxBerlin, Fabian and I worked together closely in a number of intensive sessions, spending hours transforming his research into a TED-ready talk. Together, we crafted a compelling story using different storytelling frameworks, boiling down the complex ideas into simple messages.

1.2 Mind Map

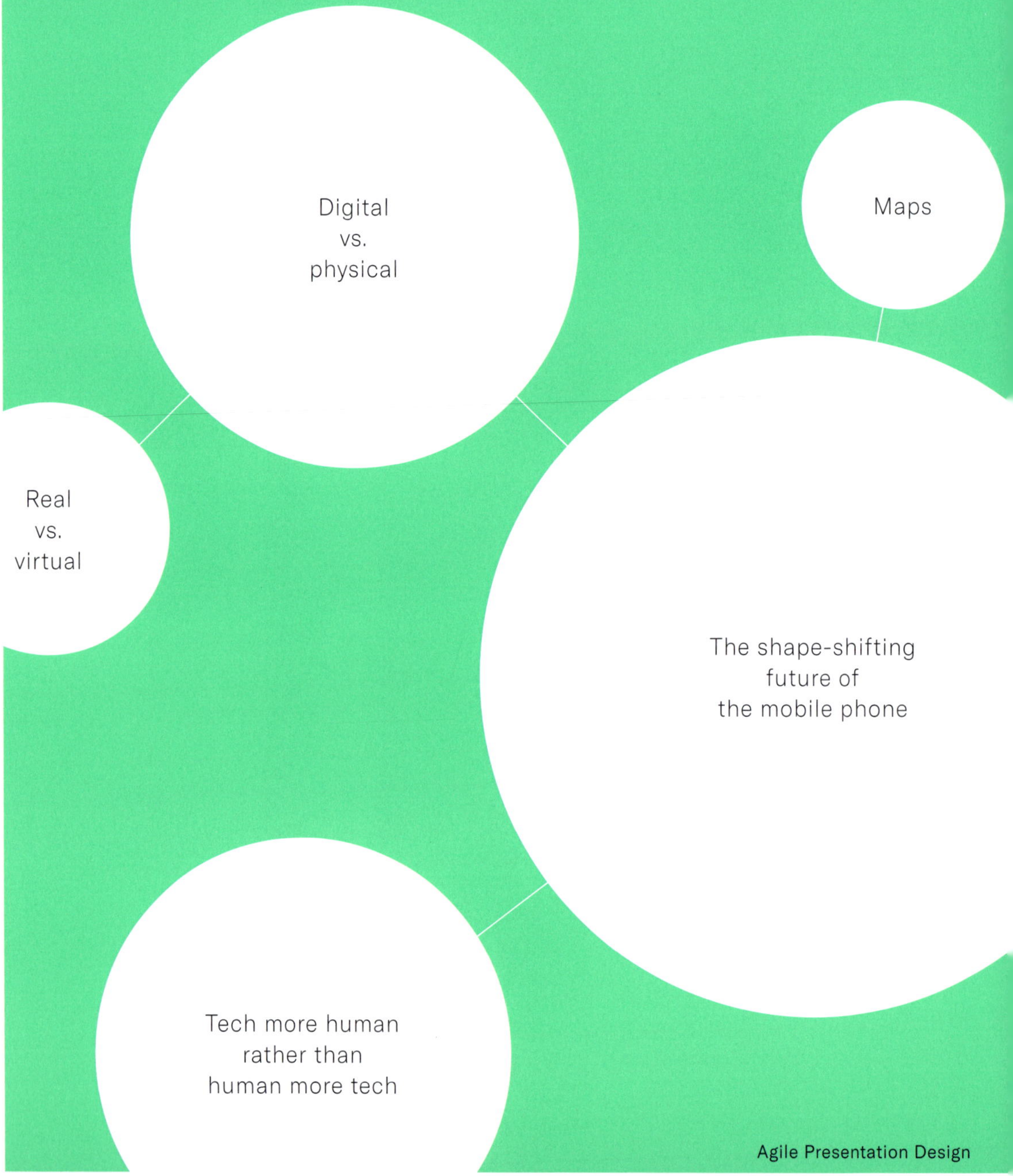

Digital vs. physical

Maps

Real vs. virtual

The shape-shifting future of the mobile phone

Tech more human rather than human more tech

Agile Presentation Design

A MIND MAP is a way of getting to the heart of a topic by building upon associations. Creating a mind map helps shape all the ideas for your presentation into a clear, logical structure. The first step to mapping is something we call the brain dump. This means getting all your ideas—no matter how rough they may be at this point—out of your head and onto paper. Or in this case, onto sticky notes. Start by setting a timer for five minutes. Once you're ready, spend those five minutes quickly jotting down or sketching every idea you can think of for your presentation—one idea per sticky note. The goal here is quantity, not quality, so work quickly, and don't censor yourself.

Once you're finished, it's time for the next stage: digging deeper and looking for patterns and connections. Move the sticky notes around and create groupings. At the center of the mind map should be your core theme, with its sub-aspects connected around it. If you notice that a piece is missing, you can add connections on new sticky notes. The process creates its own structure – a variety of hierarchies – as you go along. Afterward, you can decide how many sub-points are worth including in your presentation, depending on how much time you have to talk and the depth of the audience's advance knowledge.

This is the mind map of Fabian's talk. He pushed the process a step further: Together, we took the Post-it notes of his map and laid them out on the floor. To rehearse his talk, Fabian stepped onto the different notes as he delivered his script, which helped him incorporate his talk on a deeper, physical level. I coined this method Story Embodiment™.

Polar Opposites 1.3

WE HUMANS PERCEIVE our surroundings via contrasts: Is something bright or dark? Analog or digital? An established corporation, or a startup? The same framework applies to any topic. Looking for contrasts helps to ascertain where on the spectrum the topic is located. Describe the polar opposites of your topic in order to fully comprehend its context. Polar opposites can also be useful for delineating your presentation's content into hierarchies.

Agile Presentation Design

Polar Opposites Worksheet

Identify contrasts within your topic to deepen your understanding of the context.

_____ vs. _____
_____ vs. _____
_____ vs. _____
_____ vs. _____
_____ vs. _____
_____ vs. _____
_____ vs. _____
_____ vs. _____
_____ vs. _____
_____ vs. _____

Example: Human-machine interaction

TECHNOLOGY	HUMAN
DIGITAL	PHYSICAL
VIRTUALITY	REALITY
IMMATERIAL	SENSORY
RATIONAL	EMOTIONAL
STATIC	DYNAMIC
ARTIFICIAL	ORGANIC

Beyond The Obvious

Future Scenario   1.4

THE GOAL OF many presentations is to persuade the audience that its message, a certain potential future status, is desirable and worth striving for. To achieve this, your presentation must first explain how you came to realize that something about the status quo needed to be changed for the better, and outline how you will do it. A from-to framework immerses your audience in the process, visualizing for them the status quo, the future scenario, and which solution you'll employ to get them there.

VISUAL FRAMEWORKS

VISUAL FRAMEWORKS ARE very useful tools for both analyzing and organizing the information collected in your mind map. They function like lenses through which you can see your data in a variety of new perspectives. Which people are involved; what timeframes or spatial limitations are there; is the process a linear or circular one? All these and more are the kinds of issues that visual frameworks can address.

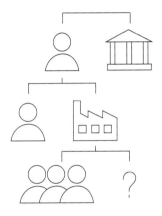

STAKEHOLDER MAP
A stakeholder map shows the various parties involved and their relationship to one other.

TIMELINE
A way to display events of the past, present and future.

PERSONA
A persona is useful when considering the goals, desires and limitations of a potential target group.

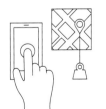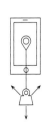

SCENARIO
A scenario puts events and actions into sequence.

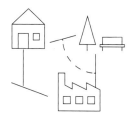

GEOGRAPHICAL MAP
A geographical map provides an overview of where things are located.

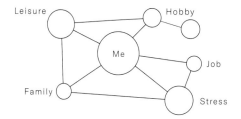

CONCEPT MAP
A concept map is a way of depicting relationships between ideas, images or words.

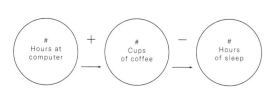

CAUSAL MAP
A causal map is a type of concept map in which the links between nodes represent causality or influence.

LINEAR PROCESS MAP
Linear process maps depict the progress of sequential steps in a flow or process.

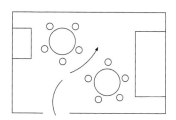

FLOORPLAN
A floorplan shows the relationship between rooms, spaces and physical features at one level of a structure.

CIRCULAR PROCESS MAP
A circular process map represents stages and actions in a sequence making a circle within a timeframe.

2-BY-2 MATRIX
The 2-by-2 matrix examines an issue along two different dimensions, representing a 4-quadrant model.

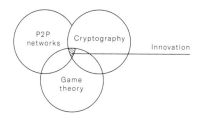

VENN DIAGRAM
A Venn diagram shows all possible relations between a finite collection of different sets.

Future Scenario Worksheet

What is the future scenario you envision?
Describe the current status quo, the potential future and how you will get there.

1 From

Start by describing the current situation.
In bullet points and visually.

_____
_____
_____
_____
_____

2 To

Now start explaining the desirable future scenario you want your audience to believe in.

_____
_____
_____
_____
_____

FABIAN USED A SCENARIO TURNED TANGIBLE PROTOTYPE TO SHOW A POTENTIAL FUTURE OF THE SMARTPHONE.

3 How

Now write out the steps and strategies you'll use to reach that desirable future scenario.

_____
_____
_____
_____
_____

Core Message

1.5

YOUR CORE MESSAGE is one single sentence that contains all the essential elements of your idea. Each word should be precisely the right word in precisely the right position. The core message contains the essence of your presentation and will help bind together the structure and content that are to follow. The facets of your core message will also define the various sections of the presentation you're building.

Core Message Worksheet

What is the one thing you want your audience to take away from your presentation?

1 Objective

What is your intention with the presentation? What do you want your audience to know, feel and do differently after your presentation? E.g. "I want to change my audience's perception on the implications of human-machine interaction because humans should not be forced to adapt to the constraints of technology."

I want to

because

2 Core Message

What is your special insight / observation regarding your topic? What is your suggestion on how to adapt? E.g. "As the digital and analog world merges more and more, we need to make sure that it's not humanity that becomes more technological, but technology that becomes a bit more human."

As...

we need to...

3 Iteration & Visualization

Iterate on your previously defined core message. Try to find a simple visual representation of that sentence.

Beyond The Obvious

"In structure, everything happens because of another."

Lew Hunter

Well done!

You've just finished the first important step in creating a compelling story. You'll see that a lot of the ideas that popped up will find their way into your presentation. Perhaps it was tough work, but I see it like Eisenhower did: "Plans are useless, but planning is indispensable."

In the next chapter, we'll build on the great work you've done so far. From here on it's about bringing your core message to life.

Can't get enough?

Books

STORY
Robert McKee. A must-read from one of the most sought-after screenwriting lecturers around the globe.

TED TALKS
Chris Anderson. The official TED guide to public speaking.

MADE TO STICK
Chip and Dan Heath. A classic on the efficient communication of ideas and why some ideas thrive and others not.

GETTING TO YES
Roger Fisher. The Harvard professor shares his insights on successful negotiation. Also great for presentations.

Links

5 STEPS TO IMPROVE YOUR PITCH
Ole Tillmann. An article for the blog of the Axel Springer Porsche startup accelerator APX. https://apx.ac/blog

THE CLUES TO A GREAT STORY
Andrew Stanton is the writer behind all three "Toy Story" movies.
ted.com/andrew_stanton

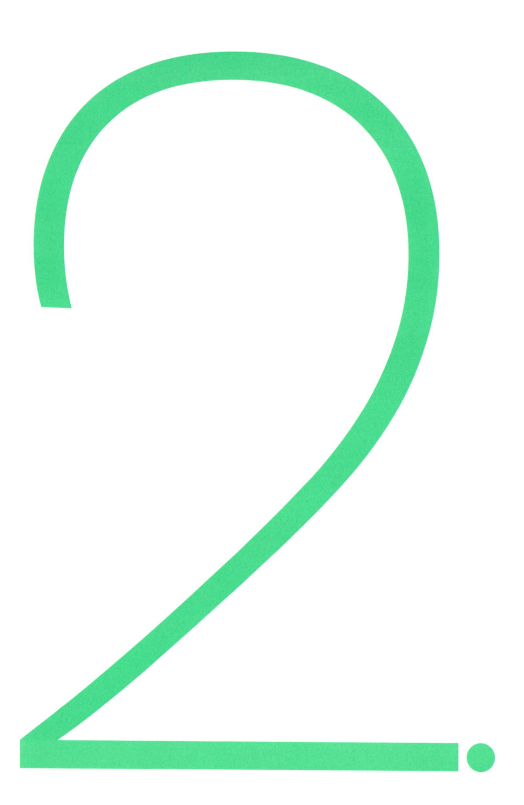
Agile Presentation Design

Chapter Two   Design

Every story has a beginning, a middle and an end. But it's everything in between that brings the story to life. There are infinite ways to tell a story. The setting and pace are just a few of the factors that shape how a story unfolds. So are the narrative components or visual devices chosen, not to mention the personality of the story's teller – you. This story-crafting process, or story design, is where your presentation comes to life – from idea to storyboard to finished slides. To best deliver your presentation's unique message, the storyline and your slides must be carefully crafted. Story design is an iterative process, one that requires an investment of many hours. But it's time well spent. It's a process of value creation in itself. A well-designed presentation is compelling, engaging and persuasive, one that will resonate in your audience's minds for a long time to come.

1	2	3	4	5	6	7
Narrative Components	Rhetorical Devices	Story-board	Outline	Script	Slide Design	Handout
p. 100	p. 106	p. 112	p. 134	p. 135	p. 138	p. 146

A good presentation weaves all relevant components into a unique storyline.

2.1 Narrative Components

1 — ANECDOTE

Anecdotes are a powerful way to illustrate your idea and bring it to life. An anecdote is a short story, such as a narrative of an experience that you or somebody else had. The meat of an anecdote – its plot – consists of an action, a subsequent reaction and then a moment of reflection when what happened is evaluated. To make use of an anecdote for your presentation, the moment of reflection should be related to your core message.

2 — USER STORY

User stories are a crucial tool in agile software development. They describe a product or service from the perspective of the user or customer. Beyond their purpose for product development, user stories can also be used in pitches or marketing materials to show the impact a piece of technology has on a person's life. This approach can make even the most complex technology understandable. And as a human being is at the center of the story, it also adds an emotional dimension, clearly demonstrating the value the product creates.

3 — EXAMPLE

Giving an example is often the first way people try to explain something. When describing agile processes, you could illustrate the concept with the example of a startup that creates an initial minimum viable product (MVP), tests it with some real customers, then integrates the feedback into the next version of their product. Examples are the most powerful way to explain something. Use them as often as you can.

4 — STATEMENT

Statements are great! They are a very useful component for your talk. Statements can be bold, punchy, personal, provocative, inspiring and so much more. You can use a statement as an opening beat, or mix them throughout your other content. Think of a statement as something people can quote you on. It could be an observation or a memorable catchphrase. It could also be a hypothesis that you go on to prove through the rest of the presentation.

Elements that will bring your core message to life

5
DATA

A good presentation balances emotional storytelling with data. Psychologist Daniel Kahnemann coined the phrase "Story over data" – meaning, raw facts alone don't persuade. Extract the relevant conclusions of your data, wrap the facts in a story and make them as tangible as possible. This is where data visualizations come in handy. Integrate bar or line graphs, pie or bubble charts, animated graphics, or simply typographical visualizations into your presentation. The options are numerous – just make sure your visuals are relatable.

6
RESEARCH INSIGHT

It's a no-brainer, but if your project involved research, make sure to include the most significant insights in your presentation. Keep in mind that it's easier to understand research results if you also show how you arrived at them. Consider sharing impressions you had during the research, telling what motivated your decisions and showing video snippets of user interviews. This helps make your conclusions more tangible for your audience.

7
SCIENTIFIC STUDY

Scientific studies can help support your observations, hypothesis and opinions and lend credibility to your presentation. Did you know, for example, that the two sleep scientists Jenkins and Dallenbach found that sleeping produces a memory retention benefit of between 20–40%, compared to the same amount of time spent awake? Interesting, right? Scientific studies show that you have done your homework and are a great way to let experts speak on your behalf.

8
THEORETICAL MODEL

Our brains are hardwired to recognize patterns. Great minds all around the world package their wisdom and expertise in frameworks and theoretical models. Using these models is like standing on the shoulders of giants. We love to cite Roger Martin, a management professor who came up with the knowledge funnel, a model that helps explain the nature of the creative process. Someone once said that theoretical models are the only way to make the vast complexity of the world fit into our tiny brains.

9   10   11   12

QUOTE   **PRODUCT DEMO**   **FUTURE SCENARIO**   **TRENDS**

Quote

Quoting other people can help the audience see your idea or one aspect of it from a very different angle. A quote from an expert can back up your statement and point of view. Or share a quote from a user, gathered in the course of your own research. We like quotes because they can add an elegant twist to a presentation. One option is to display the quote typographically on your slides, or try out video or audio formats. Make sure to place them so they fit smoothly into your story.

Product Demo

If you want to convince people of a new product, show it to them. Let your audience experience what it feels like to use the product by guiding them through the essential steps of the user flow. If you have a variety of stakeholders, make sure to show the user flow from all sides. For example, if your product is software as a service, show the interface as it appears to the end customer, as well as the backend. A product demo can vary in detail – from basic wireframes to a polished interface. Synchronize the visuals coherently with your words.

Future Scenario

Oftentimes the aim of a presentation is to convince the audience of a desired future state. If this holds true for your presentation, paint a picture of that future as vividly as possible. This can be achieved by telling a user story or describing how systems will work better in the future once a new piece of technology is implemented. Where do you see the market going? How will stakeholders behave differently? Bring this future to life and let your audience experience its benefits.

Trends

To make a future scenario even more compelling, emphasize current trends that point towards the likelihood of your scenario. What kind of technological, societal or scientific developments are leading to your future scenario? These trends can be drawn from data points but also anecdotal stories and observed patterns. As further support, you can combine these with user stories and historical comparisons. Weave everything into a simple flow. A good way to create a consistent narrative is by starting with your end in mind.

Narrative Components   101

13   14   15   16

AUDIENCE INTERACTION   PROPS   POINT OF VIEW   MEDIA FOOTAGE

One of the most powerful ways to teach people new information is by engaging them during your presentation. There are numerous ways to do this: a yes/no-question from the stage, a brief guessing game, role play or even an exercise for the audience. If you engage your audience physically, they have no option but to fully participate in your presentation. Consider asking a question and collecting responses on a flipchart. This way, you connect with your audience and your presentation becomes a conversation.

People learn about their environment through their senses: smell, sound, vision, taste and touch. To make your idea – literally – more tangible, use props or objects that embody its character. These could be concrete or metaphorical. If you already have a product, show it. If you've built a prototype, show that. All sorts of props can bring non-tangible concepts to life. For example, I use a tennis ball to explain one aspect of the creative process, which is that you proactively need to put energy into it to achieve better results.

To make a presentation more lively and personal, it's good to talk about your own point of view. What do you especially like about the idea? Do you have any personal relationship to the topic? Oftentimes we try to objectify the topics we talk about, because we confuse objectivism with professionalism. But why can't it be personal and professional at the same time? By taking a stance and sharing your own feelings, your motivation and values come to life. This gives people the chance to connect with you on a more meaningful level.

In his TED talk, media executive Gary Liu talks about the rapid growth of the internet. He does so in a mix of anecdotes, data, personal stories and examples. Those examples are backed up with soundless video content produced especially for the talk, such as scenes of a man walking through a small Chinese village to a tofu factory. The moving images make his story very vivid. A good media mix of infographics, photos and videos help keep your audience engaged, because it changes the rhythm of your presentation.

Beyond The Obvious

Interaction is a great way to engage your audience and establish an emotional connection.

2.2 Rhetorical Devices

1 Metaphor

When it comes to making an impact, the power of a well-chosen metaphor can't be underestimated. It effectively conveys the essence of a person, object or concept by referring to something with similar characteristics.

Example
-
"Our voice is the instrument we all play."
TREASURE, 2013

2 Eutrepismus

The numbering or ordering of phrases in a list helps structure your argument more clearly, guiding your audience along your train of thought.

Example
-
"Before launching the prototype, we should consider three things: First, do we have enough beta users? Second, how will the data be collected? Third, what is our goal with this round of testing?"

3 Humor

Integrating humor into your talk is a powerful tool for two reasons: first, you reveal aspects of your character, and second, humor helps the audience relax and focus. There are various ways to use humor, such as exaggeration, surprise and sarcasm.

Example
-
"I was two years older than my sister at the time—I mean, I'm two years older than her now—but at the time it meant she had to do everything that I wanted to do, and I wanted to play war."
ANCHOR, 2011

Master these devices to transform mere words into artful speech

4 Asterismos

Think of asterismos as a little attention grabber at the opening of a statement. The word (or phrase) itself may seem unnecessary, but it subconsciously draws your listeners' attention to what comes next. Obama is an asterismos champion—his favorites are "now" and "let me be clear."

Example
-
"Now, when it comes to the economy, I said that in today's world we're being pushed as never before."

"Listen! I've got an idea."

5 Anaphora

When applied deliberately, repetition always has a strong rhetorical impact. Anaphora is when a word or phrase is repeated at the beginning of numerous sentences or sentence clauses. It tends to have a rousing, emotional effect, such as in Martin Luther King's "I have a dream" speech.

Example
-
"We shall fight on the beaches, we shall fight on the landing grounds, we shall fight in the fields and in the streets, we shall fight in the hills."
WINSTON CHURCHILL

6 Sensory Language

Using sensory language makes your speech more evocative. Language that integrates the five senses gives your audience the feeling of a firsthand experience, which leads to increased engagement.

Example
-
"We prefer voices that are rich, smooth, warm, like hot chocolate."
TREASURE, 2013

7

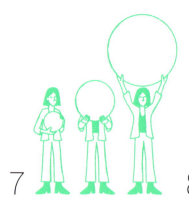

Climax

Climax refers here to a figure of speech in which words, phrases or clauses (usually three of them) are arranged in order of increasing importance – beginning with the least important and ending with the most important. It builds up excitement and highlights the most important aspect of your statement.

Example
-
"We're constantly told to lean in to work, to push harder, to achieve more."
WALDINGER, 2015

8

Metanoia

A mid-thought correction, giving the impression that the speaker is refining their thoughts and searching for the most accurate expression. It's often used to create a feeling of spontaneity or authenticity.

Example
-
"I believe—no, I know for sure—that you're going to love it."

9

Parallelism

Parallelism is when a sentence structure is repeated at least twice in a sequence. It results in a sense of symmetry and creates a resounding impact.

Example
-
"It is no longer a conversation about overcoming deficiency. It's a conversation about augmentation. It's a conversation about potential."
MULLINS, 2009

DEEP METAPHORS
Fundamental frameworks for the world around us

ACCORDING TO HARVARD professor Gerald Zaltman, deep metaphors shape the way we engage with the world. They are deep because they are universal and largely unconscious. They are metaphors because they reshape everything we think about, hear, say and do. Deep metaphors come in many variations, and often work in conjunction with one another. In this instance, think of them as a framework that can help presenters understand and connect meaningfully with their audience.

1

BALANCE
-
Balance is about the ideas of equilibrium and adjusting forces and the belief that there is a right form and order of things.

Example
Striking the right balance between financial risk prevention and risk-taking behavior to become more innovative.

2

TRANSFORMATION
-
Transformation is about changing a certain state or status into something new.

Example
The digital transformation that changes the nature of an organization.

3

JOURNEY
-
Journey is an oft-used metaphor for describing life itself. The metaphorical journey always refers to a process, like the progress people make over a certain period of time.

Example
A company on a journey, overcoming obstacles and learning from its failures.

4

CONTAINER
-
The container metaphor describes something being stored. It works in two different ways: keeping things in and keeping things out.

Example
The company name Dropbox as a description for cloud storage for files.

5

CONNECTION
-
Connection refers to the idea of belonging to someone or somewhere.

Example
Facebook uses this deep metaphor for both their company strategy and marketing efforts.

6

RESOURCE
-
Resources are related to the human instinct for survival. The metaphor always connotes something very valuable.

Example
Google's mission statement: "To organize the world's information and make it universally accessible and useful."

7

CONTROL
-
We want to feel control over our own lives. That's why this metaphor is so powerful. Even social norms exist to control the interaction within a group.

Example
Apple's marketing strategy: Giving control over personal data back to the user.

An important step towards creating a well-organized presentation is to structure the information visually.

2.3

Storyboard

Developing a narrative arc with simple sketches, text and photos

PERHAPS YOU ALREADY know that the most impressive and memorable animated movies all started out as a storyboard. First invented at Disney Studios, the storyboard soon became a standard tool in film production as a way to chart a story and share it with others. Nowadays, storyboards also play a significant role in user experience design. Companies like Airbnb, Google and Facebook use storyboards to define the customers' journey through their products, helping to make more informed decisions in product development. Whether they're comprised of rough sketches or more sophisticated designs, storyboards always communicate a story through a sequence of images.

I use storyboards as a tool to produce more effective visual presentations. Because images make your story easy to understand, a storyboard can help you share your ideas with stakeholders instantly. You can create storyboards with sticky notes, building them on the wall as early as possible. This functions as a graphic organizer to help evaluate the narrative structure of a presentation. It provides an overview of the story arc, as every part of the presentation is visible at a glance – something no presentation software can match. Another advantage of sticky notes is that rearranging the sequence as you go couldn't be easier.

The first draft of the storyboard functions as a rapid prototype. The objective is to get your ideas out of your head as early as possible. Think of the storyboard as external storage for your ideas, freeing up cognitive resources to keep honing your presentation. Once your story is down on paper, it's easy to revisit it frequently, add new ideas and take out what isn't working.

Storyboards are also a great tool to create a common understanding of an idea within a team. The visualization of the thinking process is an effective way to invite others to step in and collaborate on a story. It keeps all team members on the same page – literally. This fosters a deep sense of ownership, as everyone can contribute.

THE BEST WAY TO DESIGN YOUR SLIDES IS TO START WITH PEN AND PAPER. STORYBOARDS HELP YOU ORGANIZE, ANALYZE AND SIMPLIFY YOUR CONTENT.

Even before starting on the design of your digital slides, you'll first plot the outline of your presentation – and the main events of your story – using pen and paper. Don't fret over the details – it's absolutely fine to use stick figures and rough sketches of what you're trying to convey. Our storyboards usually consist of simple drawings and a corresponding caption. Make the images the primary content – the captions should only be very brief additional descriptions. The rule of thumb is to convey one idea or message per Post-it (and later, one per slide), using one image and one very brief sentence. The storyboard can consist of illustrations, text or photos, or a combination. Whenever we come across a fitting image on the web, we print it out – a screenshot of something inspiring, for example – and add it to our storyboard.

The neat thing about working with pen right from the start is that it forces you to think deeply about your content and simplify your material. In addition, this visual method makes it much easier to internalize your story's flow, as our brains store textual and visual information in different areas. What I especially like about storyboards is that they help to organize and analyze content at the same time – turning vague ideas into solid content. Or as Robert H. McKim, one of the leaders in design thinking, once put it: "Drawing helps to bring vague inner images into focus."

BUSINESS PITCH STORYBOARD

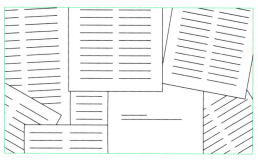

1 PROBLEM
The problem FinanzRitter addresses is threefold: too much paperwork, shady insurance brokers and cryptic pricing.

2 SERVICE / PRODUCT DEMO (SOLUTION)
The solution to this issue is an app which replaces the classic insurance broker and gives personalized recommendations.

5 MARKET
According to a study by Bain & Company, by 2020, 79% of all customers will want to manage their insurance digitally.

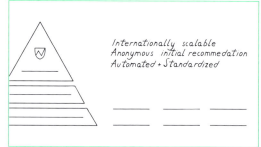

6 COMPETITION / USP
In a market this big, there is competition. FinanzRitter's USP is their machine learning algorithm.

9 ROADMAP
2016: Complete closed beta tests. 2017: Launch fully functioning product. 2019: Expand to other European countries.

10 TEAM
Dominic – CIO. Sebastian – CTO. Till – CPO. Florian – CEO.

Agile Presentation Design

This is an early draft of the pitch of insurtech startup FinanzRitter

3 BUSINESS MODEL
The service is free for the customer and FinanzRitter gets paid by recurring commissions from the insurance companies.

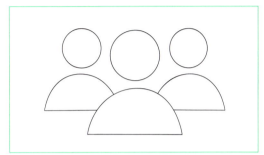

4 CUSTOMERS
The initial target group: digitally connected young professionals.

7 TRACTION
A first mockup of the app is ready and FinanzRitter is doing user and market research to validate its product market fit.

8 VISION
The vision of FinanzRitter is to scale globally and become an independent lifelong partner to its customers and partners.

11 FINANCIAL PLANNING
To establish FinanzRitter, they are asking for a seed investment of €500,000 for marketing, staff, IT and business equipment.

12 CALL TO ACTION
FinanzRitter plans to revolutionize the insurance broker experience. The team invites investors to be part of their journey.

BUSINESS PITCH STORYBOARD

1 BIG PICTURE (INCL. PROBLEM STATEMENT)
What is the big picture? Why is your idea / product important? What are the inefficiencies you tackle?

2 SERVICE / PRODUCT DEMO (SOLUTION)
How does your service or product work? What is the value proposition? What are some use cases?

5 MARKET
How big is your addressable market? Why is it a great investment opportunity? Why now?

6 COMPETITION/ USP
Who are your competitors? What's your competitive advantage? What are your unique insights?

9 ROADMAP
What are your next steps? (e.g. product development, building your organization, go-to-market)

10 TEAM
Why are you the best team to execute this plan? What's your professional background? What are your team members' roles?

Agile Presentation Design

Storyboard

Name of the idea / startup _____

_____

One-liner (Name of your startup + Customer-related verb + Customer segment + Job to be done + Your service or product)
Example: FinanzRitter is an insurance broker app that enables millenials to get optimal insurance coverage right on their phones.

3 BUSINESS MODEL
How do you plan to make money with your idea? What's the revenue model? What's your price plan?

4 CUSTOMERS
Who are (or will be) your customers?

7 TRACTION
What are your recent achievements? (e.g. customer base, product development, strategic partnerships)

8 VISION
What's the vision for your organization, product or idea? What's the growth potential of your business?

11 FINANCIAL PLANNING
How much money do you need to grow your business?

12 CALL TO ACTION
What do you want from your audience, and why?

Beyond The Obvious

Expert Interview   The Accelerator

Corporate accelerators can be a smart path for startups to gather support. Axel Springer, a prominent media company based in Berlin, has been a significant driver in the European startup ecosystem since 2013. They have invested in numerous startups worldwide through their accelerator programs. These programs provided founders with office space in Berlin and an investment of €50,000. Portfolio companies had the opportunity to learn, build, and grow with access to a diverse network of mentors, experts, corporations, and investors. For ten years, I supported all participating teams in crafting their investor communications through compelling stories and targeted pitch presentations.

Jörg Rheinboldt, a leading figure in the Berlin startup ecosystem and an active investor, played a crucial role in shaping the scene. In 1999, he co-founded the online auction house Alando, which he later sold to eBay, becoming the CEO of eBay Germany. In 2013, he began supporting the next generation of startup founders as the Managing Director of Axel Springer Plug and Play and later APX, a joint venture with Porsche. I discussed with Jörg what it takes to turn an idea into a groundbreaking product, how to establish a business successfully, and what is needed to convince investors.

JÖRG, WHAT DO YOU LOOK FOR IN A STARTUP'S PITCH?
We always ask the startup teams these three questions: "Why you?" "Why this?" And, "Why now?" You have to be able to explain why you are the best team or organization to execute your business idea. Then comes the idea itself. You must explain your dream and your vision as clearly as possible. Then, you must be able to translate this dream into theories, quantifiable structures and assumptions, and then eventually be able to derive objectives or purposes thereupon as well as to implement such a strategy. You have to show that you have the right feedback loops and that you customize execution persistently. The teams lead us through the most important dimensions of their ideas. To explain what they would like to do, how they aim to get there and then ask for the necessary support and network access.

WHAT ELSE DO YOU LOOK FOR?
As an investor, you look for founders whom you can trust to be able to do what they intend to. We look for complementary teams. What do they really want to do? Is it worth doing? Do we believe we should do it? Do we get an idea of how big it can be? Is it a venture case where venture capital can accelerate their growth? What do they already know? What do they not know? What do they know they do not know? When you hear a pitch and say, "Wow! I have really understood their vision. I had my own ideas about this topic, but the way they look at it, what to do with it as well as what they want to develop is much cooler than what had occurred to me." This is really good!

A SEED STARTUP HAS DIFFERENT NEEDS FROM A SERIES-A STARTUP. LIKEWISE, A SERIES-A STARTUP WOULD HAVE DIFFERENT NEEDS FROM A SERIES-C STARTUP. IN SPITE OF THIS, THE FOUNDERS MUST ALWAYS PITCH. DO THE REQUIREMENTS OF PITCHES DIFFER DEPENDING ON THE STARTUP'S DEGREE OF MATURITY?
Exactly. At the beginning we look very carefully at the team, their professional backgrounds and their track record. This is extremely important. The older a company is, the lower the team risk will be simply because the team has grown. That means the company is no longer dependent on a smaller number of people. At this stage, you need to be able to back your idea with real data and explain how you plan to scale your business. And you can show how you have done this in the past. I believe the biggest difference of all is that the more advanced a company is, the more reality there is in pitching. As an investor, we must look at what has been implemented and how much potential the business still has for growth.

WHAT TIPS CAN YOU GIVE STARTUP FOUNDERS REGARDING PITCHING? WHAT MUST BE OBSERVED?
There are two levels: delivery and content. At the delivery level, you need to ask questions such as, "How should I present myself?" "How can I engage people so they will join in and follow?" The other level, the content level, is where people present important ideas and put important information into context, to make it so that the listener instantly understands what is being said and can see the value in it.

WHAT ADVICE WOULD YOU GIVE IF YOU WERE TO CONSOLIDATE ALL THE NUMBERS, DATA AND FACTS THAT BELONG IN A PITCH VERSUS THE TOPIC OF STORYTELLING?

WE ALWAYS ASK
THE STARTUP TEAMS
THESE THREE QUESTIONS:
"WHY YOU?"
"WHY THIS?" AND,
"WHY NOW?"

If you do not have all the numbers, data and information, you will not be able to tell a story. However, if all you have are numbers and data, this is not a story but a heap of data. That could be exciting as well. But you need both. It does not work to just have one but not the other.

WHAT IS AN ABSOLUTE NO-GO FOR YOU?
When you can tell that people do not believe what they are presenting. That is a no-go. When you realize that the team does not click with each other. That is another red flag. In addition, there are always some fashionable trends such as artificial intelligence, machine learning, blockchain and so on. When these buzzwords are used, we listen carefully and try to find out what they really mean.

ONE MORE SPECIFIC QUESTION: HOW IMPORTANT IS THE PITCH'S HANDOUT?
Depending on how time-consuming a pitch is, the handout is a good way to make its contents readable. For example, by compiling the version that was presented on stage with relevant information on the speaker notes to make sure all the context is clear. Another idea is that if you want to send out a pitch, you could do it in the form of a video. In this way, you can bring your idea to life much better than through a PDF.

WHAT IS THE MOST INTERESTING PITCH YOU HAVE HEARD THAT STILL REMAINS FRESH IN YOUR MIND?
There was an elevator pitch I heard at a conference. An investor asked a founder: "What are you doing?" And the answer was, "We are making the software Madonna's DJ uses." I think that's a perfect elevator pitch. It is kind of clear what you do (software, music, quality, high-end, professional environment, good networks) and it clearly creates a desire to learn more (when you invest in companies in this industry). I found it so exciting. This very brief elevator pitch simply got me hooked.

THANK YOU VERY MUCH, JÖRG!

BASIC KEYNOTE STORYBOARD

MINUTE 0 - 1.30

Intro
What? When? Where? Who? Why?

OPENING BEAT

P

SETTING THE SCENE

P g   P 2   P 3
P 4   P 5   P 6
P 7

TRANSITION

P

MINUTE 1.30 - 5.30

Chapter I

INTRO

CT

BODY

P g
SP g   SP 2   SP 3
P 2
SP g   SP 2

OUTRO

WU

TRANSITION

P

COMPONENTS

Anecdote	User Story	Scientific Study	Demo	Audience Interaction	Media Footage
Example	Data	Theoretical Model	Future Scenario	Props	
Statement	Research Insight	Quote	Trends	Point of View	

Agile Presentation Design

A framework for easily creating the outline of your next talk

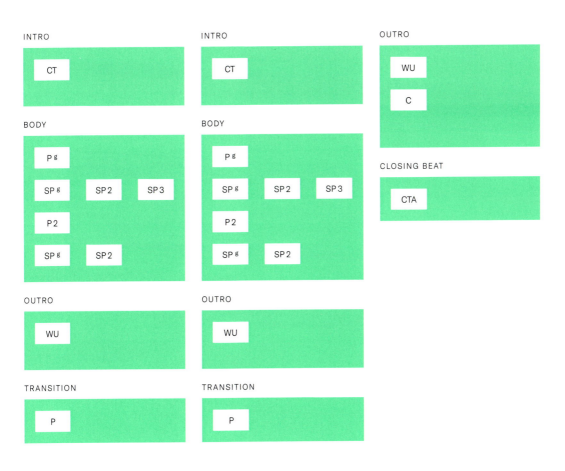

STRUCTURE

OB = Opening Beat
P = Point
T = Transition

CT = Chapter Title
SP = Sub-Point
WU = Wrap-Up

C = Conclusion
CB = Closing Beat
CTA = Call To Action

Beyond The Obvious

Illustrations in their simplest form can help to get to the core of an idea.

"Drawing helps
to bring
vague inner images
into focus."

Robert H. McKim

DRAWING BASICS

For a storyboard you don't need perfect drawings –
simple sketches are enough.

Start quick and dirty.

You don't need more than the following five shapes.

Storyboard

WORK

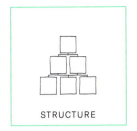
STRUCTURE

SKILL

BUDGET

PLANNING

TRAINING

SPECIALIST

COSTS

These are some icons that translate words into images.
Can you see how they're formed from the five basic shapes?

DATA

BACKLOG

PERFORMANCE

STRENGTH

PROFITS

CUSTOMER CARE

TARGET

CHANNELS

STRATEGY

COLLABORATION

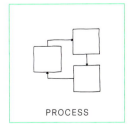
PROCESS

PRODUCT OWNER

CONCRETE ICONS

You can depict objects in a very simplified way by showing their core characteristics.
Give it a try and draw the following terms using just the five basic shapes.

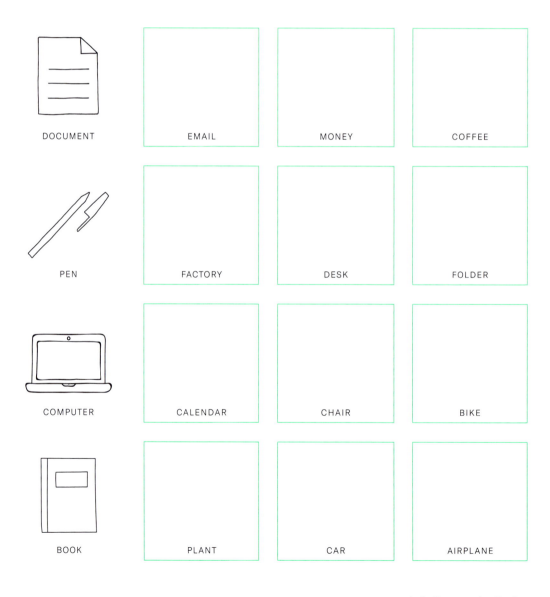

Agile Presentation Design

METAPHORICAL ICONS

There are also more abstract terms, ones that describe a concept rather than an object. Visualizing them can feel like more of a challenge. Now it's your turn: Try to find a visual translation for the following terms.

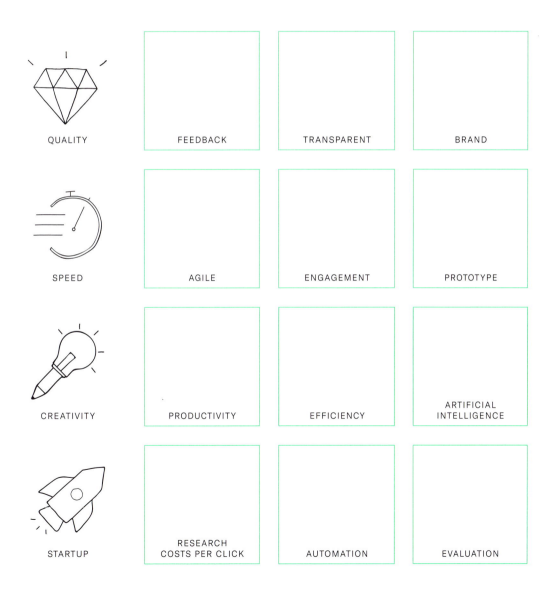

ICON LIBRARY

Agile Presentation Design

After completing those first exercises, you might already have some icons to use for your storyboard. Now we would like to encourage you to create your own personalized collection of icons. What objects or concepts are important for you and your presentation, and how could they be expressed visually? Use the boxes below to write down the terms and draw their visual translations.

2.4 Outline
Describing the structure of your presentation

YOUR STORYBOARD WILL lead you very naturally to the logical structure of your outline. The outline is a description of the creative concept behind your presentation. It should be written in a form that describes the meaning of the different parts, so that third parties can picture the presentation in their mind. At the beginning of the creative process you might have quite a long text. Try to narrow it down iteration over iteration to find the right words and their correct order. But writing alone will only bring you so far. You also need to speak your outline out loud. Try to get it to a point where you can remember the outline by heart.

First, FinanzRitter is introduced with a one-liner. Then the current status quo and problems of the insurance industry from a customer's point of view will be described.

After the dimensions of the problem are laid out, the solution is shown with a product demo of selected functions of the app.

Next, the business model is described: The user can be rewarded with 5% cash back for remaining claim-free. With a joke it is explained that all service is at no cost for the user, since the business model works through a recurring commission fee for the insurance companies. By explaining that this is an incentive for FinanzRitter, the purpose of the company is shown.

Then the target group gets introduced. The need of this target group is underlined by a study published by Bain & Company. That leads to a market volume of €10 billion and shows FinanzRitter has huge potential for further growth. Worldwide the insurance market is even larger – that is indicated by the total turnover figures in the financial sector. By introducing the competitors, FinanzRitter's unique selling point is highlighted.

After that the team is introduced with positions and professional background. With a simplified roadmap the next three milestones are shown. Based on these milestones the financial planning is explained.

At the end, the audience gets invited to become part of that journey.

Script 2.5
All your words written out

WHEN YOU HAVE finished the first draft of your outline, start working on the text of your speech. Word by word. But it's not about memorizing this text. This exercise should help you to think through your ideas more precisely. At the end, this text should read like an article in a magazine or newspaper. By the way: Have you ever thought about publishing the text of your presentation as a blog post?

"I will sit there for 15 minutes to make it one syllable shorter."

Jerry Seinfeld

Slide Design

2.6

Visual storytelling is a powerful way to get your message across

VISION PLAYS AN enormous role in how we understand our environment. Between 80–90% of the information processed by our brains is received through our eyes. When the eyes are open, an incredible two-thirds of the brain's activity is devoted to vision. Our brains are optimized to consume images and have a remarkable storage capacity for visual information. Your presentation should take advantage of these capabilities: Deliver your messages visually to make them stick.

Visual content is not only processed quicker, but remembered better, according to a study by the US Department of Labor. The result: After a solely oral presentation, the audience remembered only 10% of the content. With a solely visual presentation, it was about 35% – and when both the visual and auditory senses were engaged, the audience retained 65% of the presentation.

IN PUTTING TOGETHER your storyboard, you have already completed the preliminary step for your slide design. When translating the storyboard into digital slides, it's important that the content on your slides remains minimal. Your slides shouldn't be self-explanatory! They should just convey the key messages and support what you, the speaker, will say. Remember: just one message per slide. Your audience shouldn't be forced to read too much. A sentence should consist of around 5–10 words. When a more complex concept is being explained, it's a good idea to animate that slide. The relevant element should be timed to appear at the exact moment you talk about it. I know you may also need to give your audience a handout afterwards. No worries: I'll cover this soon.

Slide Design   137

STORYBOARD   SLIDE DECK

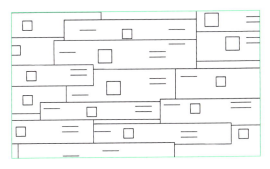 

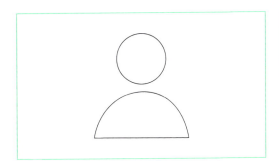 

 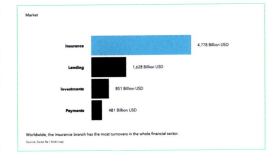

Beyond The Obvious

One idea or concept per slide.

VISUAL DESIGN BASICS

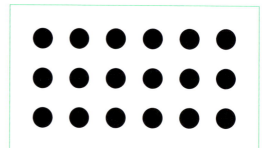

The following principles of visual design will help you to design better slides

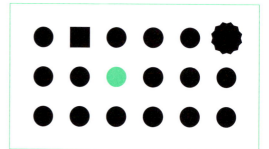

CONTRAST

We humans perceive our environment through contrasts. Contrasts can even feel pleasant for our eyes. That's why stylistic elements that create contrasts are of huge importance for design principles. Contrasts are created by elements that are very different from one another. This leads to one specific element standing out and attracting attention. Contrasts can be created through size, form, color, proximity and movement.

VISUAL WEIGHT & DIRECTION

When designing a slide, decide where you want your audience to look first. The more an element attracts the eye, the greater its visual weight. The color red tends to attract the eye more than blue, and larger elements attract the eye more than smaller ones. You should also guide your audience's eyes to the next elements. This is called visual direction. To achieve this you can use shapes, movement, arrows and lines, for example. The human eye naturally follows a line to its end.

FOCUS

Picture a billboard. Poster design is a very good source of inspiration for designing good slides. A poster aims to grab the attention of passersby, which is why its message must be simple and easy to understand. Oftentimes, a poster will have a strong key visual at its center, with simple typographic messages around it. The same principle works for your slides: Show only one aspect or concept on each. When presenting a figure, highlight the number with increased size and provide context through smaller, explanatory text.

WHITE SPACE

"White space" or "negative space" refers to the space between or around an element, such as the space between images, typography, icons or other components of your slide. White space can be used to strengthen impact and clarify important information. Though it may sound contradictory, white space doesn't necessarily need to be white – it can be any color. The space is a way to give other visual elements breathing room. For effective design, the basic rule remains: Less is more!

HIERARCHY

Visual hierarchy is the organization and prioritization chosen to communicate your content as effectively as possible. The most important message should stand out above the other information. In order to do this, you have the whole design toolbox at your disposal. Consider using a bigger or bolder font, strong contrasts, positioning or contrasting colors to create a visual hierarchy. This principle is not only important within individual slides, but for the overall structure of your presentation.

DON'T WORK JUST WITH COPY DON'T WORK JUST WITH COPY DON'T WORK JUST WITH COPY DON'T WORK JUST WITH COPY DON'T WORK JUST WITH COPY DON'T WORK JUST WITH COPY DON'T WORK JUST WITH COPY DON'T WORK JUST WITH COPY	

MEDIA MIX

The human brain loves patterns – but if patterns are used too frequently, your audience tunes out. That's why you should make sure to create a varied design. You can draw some of your aspects on a whiteboard, for example, and collect feedback from your participants. The more interactive your presentation becomes, the better. To create some variation in your slide design, you can use infographics, but also photos, videos, typographic information or illustrations. Develop a feeling for the right balance of different content formats.

CONSISTENCY

Variety is beneficial for your presentation. Still, you should make sure your presentation is visually consistent. This will make your content even more understandable. By using the same visual language throughout your presentation, you create coherence. That's why you should define certain visual aspects right at the beginning, such as the style of your headlines, how you include photos or how you use colors and shapes. Once defined, you should follow these throughout the design of your presentation.

Handout

2.7

The handout is a self-explanatory version of your presentation

THE HANDOUT IS a combination of your presentation's script and your slides. Place the most important elements you spoke about next to the corresponding visuals, using either continuous text or bullet points. Just remember: The handout is different from the slides used during your presentation.

When working with clients, I often come across slides intended to serve two purposes in one: for the presentation itself, and also for sharing with people who weren't in the audience. The result is slides with far too much content to work as a visual aid. The audience can either listen to the speaker or read the text on the slides, but not both – a baffling and frustrating experience.

THOUGH IT MAY require more effort, I recommend creating two separate sets: presentation slides and a handout. The former is designed for people sitting in your audience. The latter is for someone delving into your presentation later, on a computer screen or on a printout.

To keep your communication consistent, I suggest sticking to one design system, which also saves time as well. To get some inspiration on how to design your handout effectively, take a look at the product websites of large tech companies like Apple, Google or Tesla. Just like a handout, a product website needs to be self-explanatory. These websites all have a clear layout, use professional images and balance text and images in an optimal way. Applying these fundamental design principles will help you produce more professional-looking handouts.

SLIDE DECK   HANDOUT

Congratulations!

You have just built the foundation of your presentation's design. As you've seen, there are endless ways to bring your message to life. In order to create a presentation that really resonates, you need to gain as much empathy for your listeners as possible and have a clear understanding of your presentation's goal. Once your core message is set, the next step in the evolution is hammering out the concept and design of your overall content. It's important to remember that designing a presentation requires numerous iterative steps – from the first draft to the final product, trimming and polishing as you go. World-class illustrator Christoph Niemann frames his ambitious work philosophy like this: "I try to achieve a level of simplicity where, if you were to take away one more element, the whole concept would just collapse."

Can't get enough?

Books

EXPERIENCES IN VISUAL THINKING
Robert H. McKim. A fundamental masterpiece on the significance of visual thinking in the innnovation context.

GOOD CHARTS
Scott Berinato. If you want to deep dive into the world of data viz and presentation, this book is the right one for you.

99 WAYS TO TELL A STORY
Matt Madden. A series of captivating one-page comics that tell the same story ninety-nine different times.

COOL INFOGRAPHICS
Randy Krum. A practical guide that focuses on visual design techniques.

Links

YOU ARE FLUENT IN THIS LANGUAGE
Christoph Niemann talk about the power of visual thinking.
ted.com/christophniemann

PRACTICAL TIPS FOR UI ANIMATION
A talk with some neat tips on how to improve the animation of user interfaces.
youtu.be/LmXVxkWjLT8

3.

Agile Presentation Design

Chapter Three

Deliver

The stage has a very special appeal. Some people love being up there; others freak out. The moment you step in front of your audience, things can get intense. Within minutes you can either win the hearts and minds of your audience or lose them completely. To make the most of your time on stage, you should be well prepared. You want to create a memorable experience for your audience, but this is also a great opportunity to get into a conversation with them and test out your idea.

To do this, you need to connect with your listeners, finding out which parts of your concept resonate and which don't – before, during and after your presentation. Make sure to use their feedback for the next iteration of your presentation. This is how you build up a more concise version of your pitch, step by step, presentation after presentation.

This is what Agile Presentation Design is all about.

1
Rehearsal

p. 154

2
Presentation

p. 178

3
Feedback

p. 182

4
Iteration

p. 184

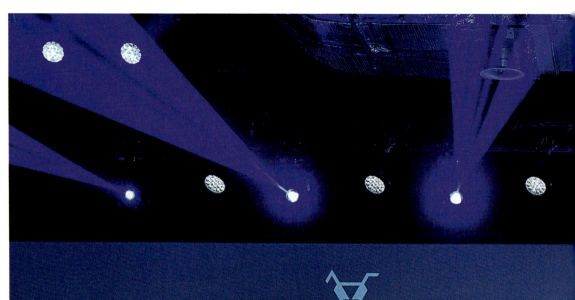

I hosted the 2017 World Web Forum in Zurich, a conference with 1500 executives from across the Swiss business sector.

Rehearsal   3.1

You owe it to your audience to be as prepared as possible

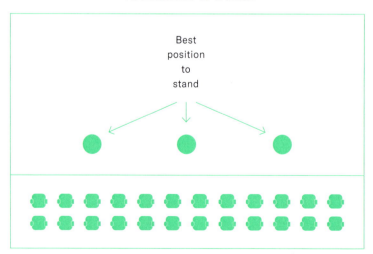

Rehearsal

THE PREPARATION IS as important as the actual presentation. Regardless of whether your audience will be 5 or 500 people, in a boardroom or a ballroom, take the time to practice, practice, practice. Rehearsing will make you more secure and relaxed on the big day. But there's also this to remember: You owe it to your audience. It's a matter of respect. You're asking the audience to give you a significant chunk of their time and attention, so you should make it worth their while.

In the days and weeks in advance of your show, rehearse as often as you can by delivering your entire presentation – out loud – along with your slides on a large screen. This is the only way to find the flaws in your story. Don't try to memorize your script word for word. Instead, internalize a sense of your presentation's underlying structure. No one wants to watch you recite. They want to experience you birthing your ideas live on stage. Though it takes work to pull this off, it will make your performance far more authentic and resonant.

As you rehearse, get a feel for your presentation slides and make sure you synchronize your words with the visuals as precisely and coherently as possible. The result should be a smoothly flowing and meaningful experience for your audience. Bring in some colleagues to be your audience and give feedback on your story, your slides and your delivery. Ask them to take notes and share them with you afterwards. As you rehearse, monitor how long your prepared presentation is taking to deliver. Even in a 5-minute pitch, you should never rush or force yourself to speak faster. If you find that what you've prepared goes over the allotted time, edit and trim your presentation rather than speaking faster to squeeze everything in.

ON THE DAY of the event, arrive early. If you're speaking at a larger conference and there's a general rehearsal, arrive early to that too. The general rehearsal will look something like this: technicians will still be preparing the lights, sound and on-stage setup. People with headsets will be running around, absorbed in the printed schedules held in their hands. It can be a pretty intimidating atmosphere. As a speaker, you'll have to tune this all out. Make the most of this important opportunity to get familiar with everything and do a complete run-through. The first thing you should do is to walk up front and get a feel for the stage and the room. Which parts of the room can you see from the stage? Is the light blinding your eyes? Where is the monitor with your slide previews? If its position needs to be changed, ask the stage manager. Are there video cameras? If yes, go take a peek at their screens. Speak to the operator about how the show will be filmed. Usually, there is one camera shooting the overall stage, and one or two cameras getting close-ups of the speaker.

WHEN IT'S YOUR turn on the rehearsal stage, own the room for that period of time. Don't be shy or unnecessarily humble. Try to run through your presentation from start to finish, including the visuals! Check that all the animations in your slides work, and the fonts are right. Get used to using the remote control. Do a proper microphone check. It's important to notice how the acoustics of the room make you sound. If you're wearing a headset, move your head left and right and see what feels comfortable. After your rehearsal, familiarize yourself with the space even more. Have a look at the stage from all the different angles. Go to the last row, take a seat and imagine how the audience is going to perceive you while you're on stage.

This may seem excessive, but it isn't. What separates the amateurs from the professionals is that the professionals take preparation and rehearsals seriously. You will have enough to worry about on the big day itself. The more time you give your brain to get familiar with being on stage, the more at ease you will be when it's time to step into the spotlight.

"The key to presence is relaxation."

Julianne Moore

PEAK PERFORMANCE
How to be relaxed and confident on stage

THE MOST SUCCESSFUL speakers are clear, confident and relaxed in front of their audience. They strike the right balance between energetic, calm and focused. Psychologists call this state of mind the flow state. Only when we're in this state can we achieve peak performance. When we're in flow, time moves imperceptibly as we become completely engrossed in a task. A speaker who is in flow comes across as absolutely in sync and in control. But being on stage can be a daunting experience for even the most accomplished presenter. Why is that? Let's have a look at the biology of nervousness.

When we hear, see or feel a real (or perceived) threat, a part of the brain called the amygdala jumps into action. It triggers the hypothalamus, the part of the brain that controls the production of the stress hormones adrenaline, noradrenaline and cortisol. The hormones are released into the bloodstream, which kicks your brain and body into survival mode. They activate the sympathetic nervous system to get your heart pumping, your blood flowing, and your muscles tensed for action – every internal function needed for "fight or flight." This is great if you need to escape a hungry tiger, but doesn't help when you're standing in front of an audience.

THIS PROCESS ALSO overrides the brain's prefrontal cortex, which controls planning, impulse control, decision making, reasoning and problem solving. More primitive impulses take over the brain – a so-called amygdala hijack. This creates an inability to adapt appropriately to highly stressful situations, as Amy Cuddy, a researcher at the Harvard Medical School, puts it. In other words: You can't keep your cool. We stay in this state of arousal until the (perceived) danger passes. Only then does the parasympathetic nervous system kick in to cool the body down, and we can finally start to relax.

But there can be some benefits to stress. It can make us more productive and focused – up to a point. According to the Yerkes-Dodson law, physiological or mental arousal leads to an increase in performance, but only up to a certain tipping point. After that, performance quickly drops.

GREAT PERFORMERS SUCH as pro athletes and entertainers know that to be ready for their big moment, they need to be able to manage their energy effectively. To get into the right zone, you need to find your individual sweet spot. People who tend to be too relaxed (yep, they do exist) need to do activation exercises. Those who are more prone to stress need to learn strategies for how to relax. The good news is: Everyone can learn how to be more relaxed on stage with some easy exercises and lifestyle modifications.

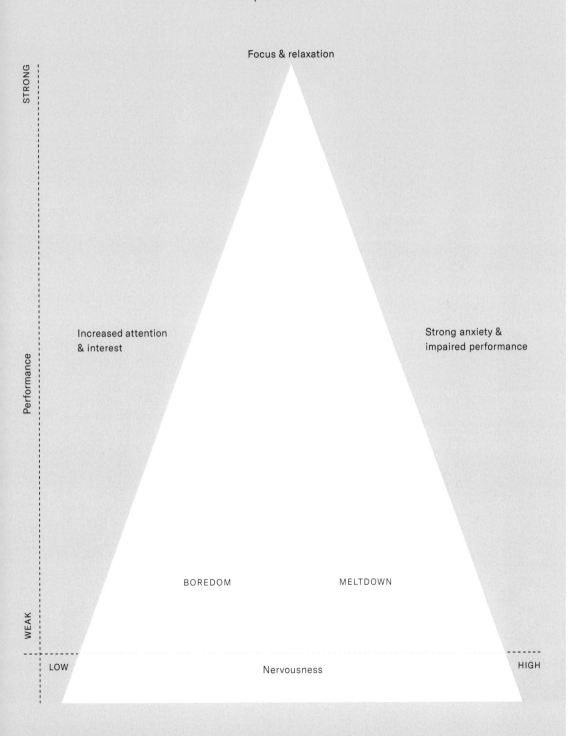

FIVE EFFECTIVE WAYS TO CALM DOWN

Everyone can learn to be more relaxed on stage

EXERCISE

Exercise isn't just for health. Regular physical activity is one of the most effective stress-reducing techniques out there. Even a few minutes of movement a day helps boost cognitive function. It's also one of the best ways to reduce stress levels before a presentation. Exercise gives the body a chance to practice dealing with stress. According to Professor Rod K. Dishman from the Exercise Psychology Lab of the University of Georgia, it forces the body's physiological systems — all of which are involved in the stress response — to communicate much more closely than usual. The cardiovascular system communicates with the renal system, which communicates with the muscular system. Exercise also produces endorphins in your brain, which leads to better sleep.

MEDITATION

Meditation helps focus and calm your mind. It has been shown in multiple studies to improve concentration by training the mind to block out distractions and focus on a single element, a skill that carries over seamlessly to your time on stage. There are various meditation techniques, most of which will help you focus on your breathing. Another great technique is body scan meditation, focusing on your body and its individual parts to pull your mind into the present moment and calm down. Because they have similar positive effects on mood and concentration, the state of flow has been likened to a kind of meditation. Training the mind with meditation will make it easier to slip into a state of flow next time you stand on stage. On Spotify you'll find a "Guided Meditation" playlist, with more than 100 tracks of calming meditations.

SLEEP

Sleep is the single most effective thing we can do to reset our brain and body each day. It also significantly improves your brain's ability to retain information: Research has shown that the more sleep cycles an individual has at night, the greater the restoration of learning ability the next morning. In one study by psychologists John G. Jenkins and Karl M. Dallenbach, it was found that sleep offers a memory retention benefit of between 20–40%, compared to the same amount of time spent awake. Sleep is also strongly connected to physical performance. If you sleep for less than eight hours a night, you will reach a state of physical exhaustion 10–30% sooner. So try to get enough sleep as often as possible, and especially the night before your presentation.

▮ BREATHING

▮ STRETCHING

A simple yet powerful exercise to quickly calm your nerves is to engage in controlled, mindful breathing for between 30 seconds to 2 minutes. According to the Harvard School of Public Health, "Deep abdominal breathing encourages full oxygen exchange – that is, the beneficial trade of incoming oxygen for outgoing carbon dioxide. Not surprisingly, it can slow the heartbeat and lower or stabilize blood pressure." Beginners should start by lying on a yoga mat on the floor. Take a long, deep breath through your nose while counting silently to three. Hold it for one second, then gradually exhale through your mouth while counting silently to six. Repeat this until you feel calm. With more practice, you can eventually do this exercise while sitting.

The mind and body are connected in myriad ways. Every thought, emotion and impulse causes a physiological reaction. Fortunately, the mind-body connection is a two-way street: Our physical actions and movements affect the state of our thoughts, emotions and impulses as well. This effect is called embodiment: the interplay of our mind and our body. With the right physical exercises, you can tap into your emotional well-being. Stretching can help activate the relaxation response, decrease stress, and release tension from your body. This sends your brain the signal that it can relax again. So next time, just before getting on stage, go through the stretching and warm-up routine that I'll show you on the next pages. Just make sure to stretch gently, and not push your body beyond its comfortable range.

Learning how to be more relaxed in your body will increase your stage presence.

"I'll do a couple of sit-ups and push-ups. That's what I do. And I stretch."

Ellen DeGeneres

A PRE-STAGE WARM-UP
Get into a balance between activation and relaxation

NO ATHLETE WOULD ever go into a competition without warming up their body beforehand. No professional comedian, singer, dancer, actor or presenter should kick off a show without properly warming up, either. The goal of a warm-up is to bring body, voice and mind to the right temperature, to release stress from the muscles and find the right balance between tension and relaxation. As you've already learned, stress delivers a big dose of the hormones adrenaline and cortisol into the bloodstream, creating tension in the body. Releasing this tension from your body gives your brain the signal that everything's alright and it can calm down. Just what you need to achieve peak performance on stage.

ANCHOR YOUR FEET
-
Our feet once had the same functionality as our hands, back before humans began walking upright. But reactivating a bit of that heritage can do us good. Feeling a connection between our soles and the floor provides the sense of stability and energy needed for a good show. Remove your shoes, take two tennis balls, and step on them. Now try to "grab" into the floor using your toes and your heel. After a minute, step beside the balls and notice the more intense connection between foot and floor. Repeat 3–5 times.

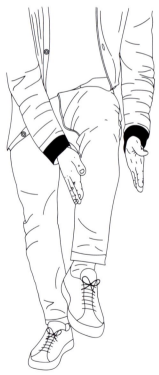

CLAPPING
-
Clap your hands over your entire body to gain a sense of physical awareness and to release tension.

Agile Presentation Design

1 Body

As a speaker, your body is an important element. Warm it up in order to be in top performance mode on stage.

STRETCHING

The entire body is involved in speech production, so it's important to warm it up as a whole. Here are a couple of exercises to energize your body and get ready to roll.

2 Posture

These exercises will help your body maintain a confident, upright stance during your presentation.

WALL STRETCH
-
This exercise improves your posture on stage. Stand with your back against a wall. Extend your hands up toward the ceiling while simultaneously lowering your bottom to the floor. Hold for 45 seconds, then walk through the room while noticing the exercise's effect on your posture.

STABLE STAND, FLEXIBLE TORSO
-
Take a soft ball and press it between your tailbone and a wall. Hold this position, actively using your feet to maintain a stable position. Rotate your torso from one side to the other to get a feeling for its flexibility.

IMAGINARY HANDS
-
This exercise will get you into an upright position both physically and mentally. Hold up both hands on either side of your body, in your line of peripheral vision. Now move them slowly backwards, until they're just at the edge of your peripheral vision. Keep holding your hands in that spot for 10 seconds. Now close your eyes and visualize your hands held up there. Put your hands down, while still maintaining that mental image of your "imaginary" hands. After 30 seconds, open your eyes. Walk around the room, maintaining the sensation of the imaginary hands the whole time.

CHAIR STRETCH
-
Another useful exercise to improve your posture. Lie belly-down in front of a chair. Raise your hands onto the seat of the chair, letting your head hang down below your arms. Stay in this position for 45 seconds. Afterwards, walk around the room again.

3 Face & Voice

Your face is the first thing your audience will look at, so it's important to have it relaxed and confident.

TONGUE TWISTER
-
The tongue is a powerful muscle and absolutely key to speaking clearly and articulately. Warm it up with a few tongue twisters.

MMMHHH...
-
1. Make a chewing motion, as if you have something delicious in your mouth. Do it for a minute or so.
2. Add some tone to the motion. First with as high a pitch as you can, then as low as you can.
3. Make an "M" sound, using this as a launch pad into the vowel sounds: A, E, I, O, U. Consonants are the gunpowder of language, while vowels contain the emotions. Combine them, and you'll be forming words.

FACIAL MASSAGE
-
Get the tension out of your facial muscles by massaging them gently for two minutes.

THE WOODEN STICK
-
As a public speaker, speaking clearly and articulately is important for maximizing your stage presence. One very effective exercise to help with this involves a simple, flat wooden stick, like the ones used by doctors. Use this stick or tongue depressor to push your tongue back gently. Now exercise your tongue by trying to speak as clearly as possible.

RESONANCE
-
Hold a soft ball about 5 cm in front of your mouth. Try to make the ball resonate by making an "M" sound with your voice. Increase the resonance gently, step by step.

THE TRUMPET
-
Relax your lips by letting them flutter. Do this for a couple of breaths at first, without sound. Next, add high and low tones, which will activate the full spectrum of your voice.

4 Breath

The single most effective way to find your focus is through breathing.

FOCUSED BREATHING
-
This exercise is a great way to finish a warm-up routine, as it gets you relaxed and focused at the same time. It also helps create awareness of your breathing, which is important, as many people forget to breathe while they're speaking. Let's go!

Stand up straight. Your feet should be shoulder distance apart. Focus your vision on an eye-level point across the room. Now breathe in as you raise your hand above your head. Form your lips to make an "F" sound, and let the breath stream out of your lips as focused as a laser beam. Exhale completely, without expending effort or pausing. As you exhale, lower your hand back down. Time it so that your arm is dangling at your side when your lungs are fully empty. Hold for 2 seconds, noticing your impulse to inhale. Now open up your throat, letting breath enter your lungs while raising your arm above your head again. Repeat the cycle 10 times. Now you're ready for the stage.

BODY LANGUAGE

How body language determines the way you're perceived

WHETHER YOU LIKE it or not, people make an assessment of you the moment you step on stage or enter a room. Subconsciously, they are asking themselves whether you're a friend or foe. To do this, they look for physical cues that reveal your intentions and your level of competence, and draw conclusions based on these initial observations. Researchers have found that these observations are made within the first seconds of meeting someone. It is in this moment that we decide how much we like or dislike someone, whether we trust them or not, and whether we perceive that person as being, for example, warm, friendly, competent, dominant or nervous.

This quick decision-making process in our brain is known as thin slicing. Often, people will continue looking for information that supports their first impression of a person, rather than information that would call that assessment into question. This effect is called confirmation bias and highlights the importance of making a good first impression. The good news is, you can prepare for making a good impression if you understand how these subconscious judgments work. Think of it as nonverbal communication. Learn how to use physical cues to make your audience perceive you the way you want to be – in a way that supports your presentation's message.

To come across as trustworthy and competent, master the following body language attributes:

RELAXED
-
Your posture should signal relaxation; avoid hectic movements.

STABLE
-
Have a stable position, with a good feel for the floor. Avoid happy feet – purposeless movement of your feet. Stay flexible in your knees.

CLEAR
-
Make only the necessary movements and gestures to support what you're saying. When speaking to someone, make eye contact and let your body completely face the person you're talking to. Make your intentions easily readable for your audience.

FLOATING
-
Your movement and gestures should have a floating character. Try to avoid quick and jerky movements.

DYNAMIC
-
Use your hands to support your message; don't be too stiff. Keep moving and bring energy into your gestures.

WITH TIME AND practice, we can improve what our body language communicates to others. The brain has a great capability to rearrange its neural pathways, what scientists call neuroplasticity. Through repetition, new behaviors are internalized and come to feel natural over time.

But don't try to change everything once. Pick one thing to work on at a time – actively using your hands while speaking, for example – and stick with it for a while. Once this has become second nature, pick the next thing to work on.

Before you know it, you'll be a natural at nonverbal communication.

HOW TO STAND
And what to do with your hands

CHIN

Parallel to the floor; not too high, not too low.

CHEST

To create presence, expand your chest slightly, taking on the room. Show, don't hide.

HIP

Your weight should be carried equally on both sides, which conveys that you are well balanced.

POSTURE

-

Stand up straight, as if there is a string connecting your head and the ceiling. Your weight can be leaned slightly towards the tip of your shoes.

STANCE

Your feet should be stable, your shoulders wide and expanded. This conveys stability and openness.

FACE

It's the first body part people see, and where they look to assess your intention. It should be relaxed. You're allowed to smile!

HANDS

Your hands can be angled open in front of you, fingers slightly touching each other. This shows that you have nothing to hide and that you can tackle things.

KNEES

Make sure your knee joints stay flexible. This conveys activeness and adaptability.

Body language is imagination turned into physical movement.

Presentation

3.2

10 strategies for a better stage performance

THE BIG DAY of your presentation has finally arrived. Here are a couple of tips that will help you make the most of your precious time on stage.

g. EMBRACE THE LEADERSHIP MOMENT
-
While on stage, you have the undivided attention of your audience – so make the most of it. This is your chance to demonstrate leadership abilities, get support for your ideas and build your personal brand. Make such an impact that your audience will leave wanting to share your ideas with others. The more structured, present and approachable you come across, the better. Your job on stage is to provide clarity and value for your audience. Embrace that role and be a leader!

2. CONNECT WITH YOUR AUDIENCE
-
An effective and meaningful presentation is about the audience, not the speaker. To find out what resonates most with your listeners, connect with them as soon as possible. Your presentation begins the moment your audience enters the room. Try to engage in some small talk with them and then transfer this conversational style onto the stage. Think of your presentation as a conversation in which you have the privilege of doing most of the talking.

3. LEAVE ROOM FOR CONVERSATION
-
As mentioned above: A good presentation is a conversation with your audience. So if you ask a question, wait for the response – even if that means a moment of awkward silence. You can be confident that your audience will respond if you give them time to do so. And if your listeners pose a question, answer it sufficiently before getting back to your concept. It's a good idea to plan in a couple minutes for this kind of audience interaction.

4. STAY IN EXPLORATION MODE
-
Even though you're the one in charge, stay open to the reactions of your audience. While speaking, look for signals that your audience is still listening and following along. You will be perceived as more present if you respond to their nonverbal cues. Strike the right emotional balance between focusing on your agenda and staying open to signals from your audience.

5. FORGET YOUR SCRIPT AND JUMP

Stepping onto a stage and giving a talk is a risky endeavor, no question. For this reason, many speakers look for anchors that provide a sense of stability – a well-prepared script, for example. But repeating a memorized script is neither entertaining nor compelling for your audience. Think of it like this: If you go to the theater to see Hamlet, you don't want to see an actor perfectly citing Hamlet's lines – you want to see them embodying the role. The same applies to your presentation. Don't cling to your script for dear life. Go all in, trust in your preparation and move smoothly from moment to moment.

6. OWN THE ROOM

Even though your presentation should have the feel of a conversation, you still need to guide it with a steady hand, like a captain steering a ship. A good trick for feeling more comfortable in front of larger groups is to treat the venue as if it were your living room. But remember – you have to maintain command of that room. If you're too passive, someone else will step in to fill this gap and you'll lose control.

7. TAKE YOUR TIME

If you rush, your audience will have a hard time processing what you're saying. Take your time while describing your ideas as simply and succinctly as possible. Using down-to-earth language supports more organic communication, allows for natural breaks in the dialogue, and will help you find your individual speaking rhythm. Remember: Public speaking is public thinking. The time it takes you to think through your content is the natural length of time it will take your audience to process this information.

8. USE CLEAR, DYNAMIC BODY LANGUAGE

Every movement you make on stage communicates something to your audience. The most effective speakers harness the power of body language to support the message they want to convey. Though the aim is to move actively on stage, take care not to push it into overacting. Guide your audience with clear and dynamic movements.

9. STAY ROLE-FLEXIBLE

A good performance has a lot to do with the speaker's ability to show a broad spectrum of their authentic personality. Let's take former US president Barack Obama as an example. Within just one speech, he can embody the role of loving dad when talking about his daughters, stately politician, and comedian telling a funny joke. All of us contain a range of different character traits and roles. The ability to act authentically within those roles and to switch between them, depending on the context, adds authenticity and individuality to your presentation.

10. HAVE FUN

Talking about business doesn't necessarily mean staying deadly serious all the time. There's no need to speak as if you're at a funeral. Show your passion! Allow yourself to smile, be enthusiastic and to use informal language. Humor is such a strong weapon in a leader's arsenal because it makes you delightful to listen to, even if your content involves dry number-crunching.

INTERNALIZE THESE TIPS and you're sure to become a better stage performer. But remember, none of these strategies are set in stone. Trust your gut feeling and unlock your creative confidence. Staying true to yourself is a powerful way to connect with your audience.

After the presentation, take a moment to congratulate yourself on all your hard work. Then it's time for the next important step: harvesting the feedback of your audience.

Feedback

3.3

The real gold of the presentation design process

A PRESENTATION IS never set in stone. It is an iterative, creative product that should be fine-tuned as many times as possible over its lifetime. Each time you share your presentation with a new audience, something magical happens: your listeners respond to your ideas with ideas and associations of their own. Capture this feedback carefully, as it will help make your presentation even better for the next time.

COUNTER-ARGUMENTS
-
Although this kind of feedback can be hard to take, counter-arguments against your ideas may contain extremely valuable insights to improve your concept. Of course, your aim should always be to give your audience the fewest possible grounds for counter-arguments. While designing your presentation, always try to anticipate potential counter-arguments in advance!

QUESTIONS OF UNDERSTANDING
-
Pay close attention to what your audience asks you to clarify, as these questions highlight which points in your presentation may still be too vague or confusing. Remember, the audience comes at your content with fresh eyes, enabling them to notice issues you might have overlooked.

THEORETICAL MODELS
-
People use different theoretical models and patterns to explain to themselves the complexity of the world. A business analyst might use different models than a UX designer or an engineer. Notice what theoretical frameworks your audience members refer to when responding to your presentation. These can open up new possibilities for explaining your concept from different perspectives.

OPPOSED THESIS
-
We all have different ways of understanding the world, informed by our uniquely individual life paths, skills and experiences. As a result, it's possible that listeners may fundamentally disagree with the core thesis of your presentation. Learning how to integrate viewpoints opposite from your own will make your idea more convincing to wider, more diverse audience groups.

EDUCATIONAL RESOURCES
-
People love to share what they already know about a particular topic. Take note of any favorite books, speakers, podcasts or videos your audience members mention, as these resources may well be eye-opening for you too.

Remember: Whatever response your listeners give, all feedback is nothing less than pure gold. This is why we advocate sharing your content with people as early as possible. The insights you'll gather will help expose any weak points in your presentation concept and make the next version even better. Your future audiences will thank you!

Presentation Feedback Sheet

Ask for structured feedback about all aspects of your presentation.

---

1 Story
Does the presentation contain all necessary information?
How compelling, understandable and crisp is the storyline?

OBSERVATIONS

SUGGESTIONS

2 Visuals
How well do the slides convey the key messages?
Is the design consistent; are the fonts readable, and the images high-res?

3 Delivery
How well does the speaker engage with the audience?
What about pace of speaking, voice modulation and body language?

Iteration

3.4

Keep making your presentation better and better

MOST PEOPLE THINK the work of presentation design finishes on presentation day. But concluding the process at this stage means not taking advantage of the valuable, insightful feedback your audience provides. Only once you've shared your ideas with others do you learn what resonates and what does not. Maybe your audience responded with a couple of valid counter-arguments. Or perhaps they asked questions that show your presentation is not quite clear enough at certain points. All of this is incredibly useful information that you can use to iterate an even better presentation for the next time.

An iterative process is useful not only for presentation design, but in showbiz too. Before entering the spotlight at his larger shows, US comedian Chris Rock first practices his material at smaller venues, making between 40 to 50 appearances in front of live audiences to see which jokes work and which don't. "It's like boxing training camp. I always pick a comedy club to work out in," Rock says. For him, these small run-throughs are like testing sessions. The jokes that get big laughs go on to become the foundation of his routine at the larger venues.

THIS IS PRECISELY the approach that will help you design more meaningful and impactful presentations. Build up a library of narrative components that resonated with your audience, like user stories, infographics, personal anecdotes, theoretical models, audience interactions and even jokes that got good laughs. These components can be rearranged and restructured, just like Lego bricks. This iterative upcycling approach is time-efficient while also continually improving the quality of your content.

Just be sure to stay honest with yourself throughout this process. There may be a certain narrative component you love, but it doesn't do anything for your audience. A presentation must always be tailored to the needs of its listeners. If an element is not providing value to your audience, leave it out.

Congrats!

That's it. The loop is closed. You've just completed the entire process of Agile Presentation Design. First, you dived into gaining a thorough understanding of your presentation's context and your audience, and defined your message accordingly. Next, you built upon this foundation to develop your narrative arc and your presentation deliverables. This preparation helped boost your confidence levels to present your idea in front of an audience. After the presentation, you gathered audience feedback, which empowered you to build an even better next version.

Perhaps this design process was more involved and took longer than you were used to. But this was just the beginning. The more often you complete this process, the more it will become second nature. The result: better and better presentations, with greater resonance and impact.

Thank you very much for joining me on this path to more impactful and meaningful presentations!

About the Author

Ole Tillmann is a Berlin-based creative director and executive coach who consults with leading companies like Google, Lufthansa, WIRED, McKinsey Digital, Soho House Group, and Airbnb. He collaborates closely with organizations, founders, and leaders, using storytelling and design to shape their futures.

At 18, he began working in television as an actor and presenter, reaching millions and receiving journalistic training from the Adolf Grimme Academy. He spent three years as an acting coach, incorporating American storytelling principles and Russian acting methodology. In 2009, he joined the TED event series, preparing over 350 speakers for TEDx conferences in Berlin, Munich, and Hamburg. He also joined the coaching team at the School of Design Thinking in Potsdam and taught at the Berlin Design Academy. For 12 years, he has run PEAK, a consultancy specializing in innovation, branding, and communication design. As a professional host, Ole presents at major conferences in design, tech, startup, and digital business in the DACH region and is a keynote speaker at international events.

Thank You

I want to say thank you to my family – my beloved wife Anita and my two lovely daughters Marieluise and Charlotte. You mean the world to me. Without your love and support this book wouldn't have become reality.

In addition I want to thank Carissa, Thomas, Jörg and Fabian for their contribution to this book. And, last but not least, my team and my external experts Hilda and Axel for supporting me in getting the book ready. Iteration over iteration. I'm really proud of the result.

Sources & Inspiration

THE WRITER'S JOURNEY
Christopher Vogler

THE DESIGN OF BUSINESS
Roger Martin

TED TALKS
Chris Anderson

MADE TO STICK
Chip and Dan Heath

GETTING TO YES
Roger Fisher

EXPERIENCES IN VISUAL THINKING
Robert H. McKim

GOOD CHARTS
Scott Berinato

99 WAYS TO TELL A STORY
Matt Madden

UNDERSTANDING COMICS
Scott McCloud

COOL INFOGRAPHICS
Randy Krum

STORY
Robert McKee

PRESENCE
Amy Cuddy

GRAPHIC DESIGN THINKING
Ellen Lupto

USER STORY MAPPING
Jeff Patton

THE SKETCHNOTE HANDBOOK
Mike Rohde

STORYBOARDS
Marcie Begleiter

CHANGE BY DESIGN
Tim Brown

THE TEN FACES OF INNOVATION
Tom Kelley

EXPOSING THE MAGIC OF DESIGN
Jon Kolko

THE DESIGNFUL COMPANY
Marty Neumeier

PRINCIPLES OF TWO-DIMENSIONAL DESIGN
Wucius Wong

DESIGN IS STORYTELLING
Ellen Lupton

HOW TO MAKE A WORLD
Ed Emberley

THE ART OF INNOVATION
Tom Kelley

BUSINESS MODEL CANVAS
Alexander Osterwalder

DRAWING ON THE RIGHT SIDE OF THE BRAIN
Betty Edwards

VISUAL GRAMMAR
Christian Leborg

RESONATE
Nancy Duarte

CREATIVE CONFIDENCE
David and Tom Kelley

FEEL THE FEAR AND DO IT ANYWAY
Susan Jeffers

DIRECTING THE STORY
Francis Glebas

THE LEADER'S GUIDE TO STORYTELLING
Stephen Denning

THE VISUAL DISPLAY OF QUANTITATIVE INFORMATION
Edward Tufte

GRID SYSTEMS IN GRAPHIC DESIGN
Josef Müller-Brockmann

VISUAL THINKING IN DESIGN
Colin Ware

THINKING, FAST AND SLOW
Daniel Kahneman

PRINCIPLES OF FORM AND DESIGN
Wucius Wong

NOW YOU SEE IT
Stephen Few

Agile Presentation Design

Imprint

PUBLISHER
-
PEAK Creative Leadership GmbH
Berlin
Germany

Mail   ole@tillmann.com
Website   tillmann.com

RESPONSIBLE
-
Ole Tillmann
Managing Director
PEAK Creative Leadership GmbH

CONCEPT / REALIZATION
-
Ole Tillmann, Creative Director
Axel Lauer, Art Director
axellauer.net

TEXT
-
Ole Tillmann

EDITING
-
Hilda Hoy, Copywriter
hildahoy.com

PICTURE CREDITS
-
PEAK Creative Leadership GmbH
Dominik Tryba
Winnie Wintermeyer
Stephen Lam

ILLUSTRATIONS
-
Christopher Delorenzo
Giulia Hartz

Printed by
PEAK Creative Leadership GmbH

ISBN 978-3-00-063024-8
(c) 2024

The content and structure are protected by copyright. Any duplication, change or spreading of information and/or data, in particular of text, text parts and pictures, requires written approval from PEAK Creative Leadership GmbH.

Beyond The Obvious

Let's stay in touch.

ole@tillmann.com

 /oletillmann